CALLED TO TEACH

CALLED TO TEACH

A Spiritual Guide for Teachers and Aides

by
Rev. Walter J. Tulley

ALBA · HOUSE   NEW · YORK

SOCIETY OF ST. PAUL, 2187 VICTORY BLVD., STATEN ISLAND, NEW YORK 10314

Library of Congress Cataloging in Publication Data

Tulley, Walter J
    Called to Teach.

    1. Catholic teachers — Religious Life. I. Title.
BX2373.T4T84   248'.88   78-7534
ISBN 0-8189-0371-6

Nihil Obstat:
Justin Hennessey, O.P.
Censor Deputatus

Imprimatur:
†James A. Hickey, S.T.D.
Bishop of Cleveland
Feb. 27, 1978

The Nihil Obstat and Imprimatur are
a declaration that a book or pamphlet is considered
to be free from doctrinal or moral error. It is not implied
that those who have granted the Nihil Obstat and
Imprimatur agree with the contents,
opinions or statements expressed.

Produced in the United States of
America by the Fathers and Brothers of the
Society of St. Paul, 2187 Victory Boulevard,
Staten Island, New York, 10314, as part of their
communications apostolate.

2 3 4 5 6 7 8 9 (Current Printing: first digit).

CONTENTS

INTRODUCTION

This is not a "how to do it" book. *Called to Teach* was written especially for volunteer lay teachers of religion, actual and prospective, but not with the view of offering a course on teaching methods, or even of giving any "helpful hints." In offering this book, I have in mind the reality of the call of God to lay volunteer teachers, a call which is special to them. Most of them are not teachers "by trade." All but a few are now engaged in a different profession or way of life. Yet all of them have felt the inner need to do something special for their parish and the young people in it. I am convinced that not only is this a call from God, and a call that demands a generous response, but that it is a call to special spiritual progress.

To try to meet the need of this spiritual progress is the purpose of this book. Hopefully, the book will assist our volunteer teachers to realize the divine nature of their call. Hopefully, it will inspire others to inquire into and even to accept the call to teach. I envision that parts at least may be used as a vehicle for prayer, private prayer and group prayer. I also envision that parts of the book may be used as the basis for group discussions, at, perhaps, teachers' meetings.

The idea of the book was originally conceived by the Sister Director of Religious Education at St. Bede's. She and I had given a series of inservice programs for the volunteer teachers of the parish. Sister gave a short course on teaching methods, and I gave a short course in theology. Much of the material in chapters three and four are taken substantially from my talks. The other chapters are intended to try to relate the special call of volunteer teachers to God, to themselves, to the students, and to others who share the burden and the privilege.

I wish to thank especially Sister Mary Avery, S.N.D., for her part in conceiving, inspiring, and encouraging the production of this book. Special thanks are due to the corps of readers and critics, who faithfully read the original manuscript, and made some valuable suggestions: Sister Mary Gesú, S.N.D., Sister Mary Evarista, S.N.D., Sister Lynn Mary, S.N.D., Mrs. Anna Mae Wilson and Mrs. Janet Sadowski. Thanks are also due to the parish secretaries, Miss Debra Prunty and Mrs. Anna Roos, for the neat and accurate task of typing.

Finally, I wish to express a sense of deep and personal gratitude to the many teachers of religion, past and present, of St. Bede Parish, Mentor, Ohio, whose dedication and need, more than any other single thing, have inspired the writing of this book. It is to these people, who work for God's honor and glory, that this book is gratefully and sincerely dedicated.

CHAPTER I
WE ARE CALLED

Saul, breathing murderous threats against the Lord's disciples, went to the high priest and asked him for letters to the synagogues in Damascus which would empower him to arrest and bring to Jerusalem anyone he might find, man or woman, living according to the new way. As he traveled along and was approaching Damascus, a light from the sky suddenly flashed about him. He fell to the ground and at the same time heard a voice saying, "Saul, Saul, why do you persecute me?"
"Who are you, sir?" he asked.
The voice answered, "I am Jesus, the one you are persecuting. Get up and go into the city, where you will be told what to do" (Ac 9:1-6).

St. Paul had it easy. Jesus left him with no doubt whatsoever that he wanted him for a certain special task. In fact, there is doubt that he left him with much of a choice. He knocked him right off his horse, and said in so many words, "Please come quietly." We see in this incident that God had a special job he wanted done, and he handpicked the one person capable of doing it.

Each of us, in some way, has received such a call. This call is a mark of God's love, first of all, a love that is infinite and eternal, unique, personal and individual. It is also a mark of his providence, in so far as he uses all of us, each in our own way, to bring about the fulfillment of his kingdom. We have received the gift of faith through others; we are all called to communicate it to others. While all share in this call as Christians, some of us are called to share it in a special way, as teachers of religion. The purpose of this book is to try to see what this call means to us personally, and to those for whom we have been called.

The whole of salvation is a history of the calls that God has issued to certain people for certain special purposes. Besides St. Paul, we may consider two others specifically, Abraham and Jeremiah.

The progressive development of God's call, as well as the full implication of it, can be illustrated in the call of Abraham. Abraham was just a "wandering Aramean," as we read in Deuteronomy (26:5). It is possible, in fact, highly probable, that he had had some previous knowledge of the one true God from some half-forgotten family tradition. As the story is told in the eleventh chapter of Genesis, God started the whole procedure by making the initial contact. Abraham did not "volunteer." Along with this first contact, God made a demand. He told him to leave his home and family, and go to a land "that I will show you." As St. Paul points out, God did not even tell him where he was going! The story is told in a rather matter of fact way, but we must realize that this was no easy task to fulfill. Abraham knew that he would never see his family again, and in fact, he never did. To the demand, however, God added a promise. He promised Abraham that he would make him the head of a great nation of people, and that through him "all nations would be blessed" (Gn 12:3). It is certain that Abraham did not understand the full meaning of the promise, but it is equally certain that there was some powerful attraction in it. Abraham immediately packed up and left.

Then came the bombshell. God called again.
"Abraham!"

"Ready!" he replied. Then God said:

"Take your son, Isaac, your only one, whom you love, and go to the land of Moriah. There you shall offer him up as a holocaust on a height that I will point out to you." Early the next morning, Abraham saddled his donkey, took with him his son, Isaac, two of his servants, and with the wood that he had cut for the holocaust (Gn 22:1-3), he set out for the place of which God had told him.

There is nothing in these simple words, related in utmost simplicity, to indicate the reaction of Abraham, shock and disbelief. There is nothing to tell of his sadness, his heaviness of heart, his slowness of foot, as he prepared that three day journey that would end with all of his hopes being shattered. All we have are the facts — and especially the primary fact of the magnificent act of obedience and love as Abraham prepared to return to God all that he had been given. And yet we are certain that there was a deep and abiding trust in God, even as he raised the knife to kill his son. This trust was not unfounded, because God was satisfied with the will. He did not need the act.

We may pause to consider the beautiful act of faith and confidence in God that Abraham made. He was convinced, even in the face of a demand that contradicted it, that God would keep his promise. But there is more to it than that. Somewhere deep inside him, Abraham knew that God was calling him to goodness. We may be sure that Abraham did not understand the full meaning of the promise, as we do, that the "blessing for all nations" would come about in the person of the Savior, yet there must have been a vision, perhaps given by God himself, of something beyond mere words, "a great nation." That this is so, we may surmise from the words of Jesus, "Your father Abraham rejoiced that he might see my day. He saw it and was glad" (Jn 8:56). Once again, he was sure of God's goodness; he knew that God's call would be to peace. Faith is confidence in the certainty of the vision given us by God. It is for this reason that Abraham is called in the first Eucharistic prayer, "our father in faith."

The call of Jeremiah emphasizes one important factor of God's call, and that is the fact of his constant guidance. Since his call is always for his own purpose, we can be sure that he will assist us in fulfilling that purpose. Jeremiah describes his own call in this way, "The word of the Lord came to me thus: 'Before I formed you in the womb I knew you, before you were born I dedicated you, a prophet to the nations I appointed you' " (1:4-5). When Jeremiah objected that he was too young, God said that was not a factor. Instead, God would be with him, speaking his own words to all to whom he was sent. "Have no fear before them, because I am with you to deliver you...See, I place my words in your mouth. This day I set you over nations and kingdoms" (1:8-9). Jeremiah's prophetic office lasted almost thirty years, thirty of the most turbulent years of Israelite history, ending with the exile in Babylon. During that time, Jeremiah suffered severe physical persecution. This was small, however, compared to the spiritual anguish of his office. Yet he tells us, that in spite of the times he desired to be free of the office, the message of God was as a fire, burning within him. Jeremiah died in exile, and in his lifetime, seemed to have failed. Yet his message was a source of hope to the exiled Israelites in Babylon for many years, a hope that was fulfilled when they were sent back to Jerusalem. Jeremiah himself stands before us, a man totally dedicated to God's will, relying on God's protection, and through all his sufferings, assured of God's presence.

God has called us, as he has called others, and our first call was to faith. We may trace the details as follows. At the beginning, as children, we just hear about God. This could have come when we were very young, from our parents, perhaps, or our religion classes. At this point our faith is really in those who tell us about God, not directly in God himself, though we recite the formula, "I believe in God." At some point in our lives, however, there comes a time of real decision. Some demand is made on us to accept interiorly this God we have so far just heard about. This could come very early in our lives. It could come in many different ways. In what ever way it does come, it is a demand made on us, spiritually. Most frequently, the demand is to choose right over wrong in time of temptation. The important point to be noticed here, however, is the basis for the choice. We make the choice for what is right because the God we have so far just heard about is calling us to goodness. From within, we feel strongly this call. This is an act of real faith. We have made the change from going along with pleasing the God we have believed in to begin to please the God we know is calling us from within. *Now*, we have begun to see God as a person, and have made our first commitment to him.

Looking at the call of God to others in the past, we see that he always gave them a gift. This is true of the call to Abraham and to Jeremiah. It will be true of God's call to us. Deep inside us there is a satisfaction in doing what is right, in knowing that we are pleasing the God who has called us. There is a joy in goodness, and a peace of mind in the decision to act according to it. We begin to experience a truth that comes to us more and more as we follow the will of God, that his call is always to peace. That peace may be yet an indefinable thing. We may not see it clearly at first, but only as a vision, just as Abraham saw God's promise only as a vision. But it is there. We realize its presence, we experience the joy.

We have said that God's call is repeated, many times, in fact. One of these calls has now come to us, the call to teach religion, to bring Christ to others. It has all the qualities of the call that we have been describing. We feel it as strongly as Jeremiah did. The demand seems great indeed, but the promise, though still only a vision, is real.

Sometimes we ask ourselves why God chose the persons he did for those special tasks. We might suppose that the patient, docile Abraham was a natural choice for the one to follow the will of God silently and perfectly, and that the firebrand St. Paul was a natural choice to spread the Gospel to the nations. But why did God choose me? When we think about the call to us to teach others, we wonder just what qualities we have that make us suitable for the task. It would be extremely naive to say simply that the answer lies in the mystery of God's providence, though ultimately, that is exactly where it is. Realistically, however, we can say that since God himself is the source of our talents and abilities, it is not beyond the level of imagination to think that he endows us with certain capabilities to fulfill the certain tasks he has for us. But there is more to it than this. God not only gives us the powers, he initiates the call. This call may not be as insistent as that of Jeremiah, whose constraint to preach the word of God was a burning fire inside him. Our call may come to us in different ways. Perhaps we have heard the appeal in church for teachers, and our conscience has been stirred; perhaps we see our own childrens' need; perhaps the whole thing is interior, a desire to share our own gift of faith. But we recognize the call as coming from God, insistent, forceful, and at times almost imperceptible. But the call is there, and it keeps coming back. And we know it is coming from God.

We also recognize the awesome task that it entails. The responsibilities, the demands it will make on our time, our patience, our capabilities. And the most difficult part of it is, we are not at all sure of ourselves. We feel ourselves kind of split down the middle. We truly feel God calling us, yet we see our own inadequacy. More specifically, these are some of the things that go through our minds that hold us back: Will I have the time, or perhaps more honestly, am I willing to give the time? Am I capable? Will I really be able to teach? Have I the power to communicate the truths of faith so that the students can grasp them? Or even more fearfully, will I be teaching, what I believe is the truth, but which actually is not? That old "bugaboo," fear, raises itself up to stand in our way. In spite of all this, however, the call keeps coming back, insistently, insistently, ever *more* insistently.

And yet in the midst of it all, somehow, we see a vision. We may not put it in these precise words, but the idea filters through. Somehow or other, we are able to see the satisfaction we will receive from teaching others. And the funny thing is, we are not deceived. There is indeed the satisfaction that comes simply from doing what God wants us to do, the simple satisfaction of knowing that we are pleasing him. There is the satisfaction that always comes to us when we are doing something for others. And this is heightened by the fact that the value we are giving here is not merely natural, but supernatural, and for that very reason, is beyond measure. And every once in a while, some student will show us some insight or understanding that we have brought to him. We will know then that all the demands, all the anxieties, all the time and effort have been well repaid. We begin to realize this truth, God's call is always to peace.

St. Augustine says that peace is the tranquility of order. The peace that we are talking about here is that interior peace of mind, peace of soul. Fundamentally, this peace comes from God himself, but it requires our readiness to put things in order within ourselves. This peace is on two levels, with ourselves, and with God. With ourselves, the order required for peace is this: that we are sure that what we are doing is right. We rest tranquil in that assurance. With God, the order required is this: that our wills are in tune with his.

Let's go back to the beginning. The whole thing starts with God, not with ourselves. And it is we whom he has chosen, in the mystery of his divine providence. It will help us to remember that God never gives us a grace just for ourselves. Our own firmness of faith, our willingness to please, our devotion to him, the sum total of our Christian living is ours because ultimately God has given us these things as a direct grace. Some of these, indeed, at least in germ, we received from others. But none of them were given to be kept wrapped up in a nice tidy little bundle hidden and protected from all others. Just as God has used others to bring goodness and devotion to us, so has he intended us to bring the same to others. God indeed has called us, and the call indeed is not easy. But the rewards, for ourselves and others, are great, for once again, God always calls us to peace.

The bishops of the world, in the Second Vatican Council, and especially in the Dogmatic Constitution on the Church, have defined the role of the Church today, as well as the roles of the different members of the Church. In the chapter on the Laity, the Fathers point out that every Christian is in some way called by God to a special three fold task, that of priest, prophet and king (nn. 24-36). The call to teach religion corresponds beautifully with each of these roles.

We share in the priestly role of Jesus by offering sacrifice. Since, however, in Christ, priest and victim are one, our share is also in being sacrificed. We may listen to these words, "For all their works, relaxation of mind and body, if they are accomplished in the Spirit — indeed even the hardships of life if patiently borne — all these become spiritual sacrifices acceptable to God through Jesus Christ" (Church, n. 34). The awesomeness of the task, with all the sacrifices it entails, can be made a part of this priestly sacrifice we make of ourselves, both as fulfilling our role as laity, and our special role as teachers. Nor should we forget the fact that we have a share in the renewal of Jesus' own sacrifice in the Mass, where he, as priest and victim, gives us the strength and grace to be one with him. Indeed, by making all of our actions holy, we may "consecrate the world itself to God" (Church, n. 34).

The normal connotation of the word 'prophet' in our modern sense is one who fortells the future. The basic meaning, and the one intended by the Fathers of Vatican II, however, is one who proclaims a message. All Christians, indeed, are called to this task. But this is the special task to which we, as teachers of religion, are called. The proclamation of the message is not in word alone. It is the communication of ourselves as true Christians. And since no one can give anything they do not have, our first task is to try to live close to Christ. We must, indeed, be the leaven that permeates the whole mass of dough.

Our participation in the royal office of Christ comes from the fact that the kingdom of Christ is now, here in the world. It involves our recognition of the inequalities among the people in the different classes of society, as well as people throughout the world. It also involves our willingness to try to do something about it. "Get involved", as the expression is today. In this, as in all other things, our role of teacher is just an expansion of our personal convictions. We communicate to others of what we ourselves are deeply convinced. Thus, the call from God demands change, the need to change ourselves, and the need to communicate change to others.

Looking at these roles as pointed out by Vatican II, and seeing the special meaning they have for us as teachers, we wonder if we have the ability to live up to them. Then we look inside ourselves, and realize that God himself has issued a call, and that call is an invitation. All we have to do is say, "Yes." When we do, there is no way that we will ever be able to count our blessings that will come to us. More importantly, however, there is no way that we will ever be able to count the value to others, to those whom God, in his marvelous providence, has intended us to serve. God's call is an invitation — an invitation, to be sure, that involves a sacrifice. But it also involves a promise, a promise that will be fulfilled for us, and wonderfully fulfilled for others.

We come, finally, to a consideration of God himself. Who is this God who calls us to this special task? In other words, what is God like? All of us have grown up with different images, as it were, of God. He is described in the catechism as a "spirit, infinitely perfect," with all the attributes of power, eternity. We have been taught that he is the supreme and perfectly just judge, who will reward and punish each as we deserve. Neither of these images, nor others, need be untrue, but it does help if we have a correct image of God who is calling us.

The readings for the feast of the Holy Trinity, cycle

B, give us three images of God. In the Gospel (Mt 28:16-20), Jesus speaks for the first time what we may call the Trinitarian formula, "the Father, the Son, and the Holy Spirit." God in this aspect is the Ineffable, the Incomprehensible, the God of infathomable mystery. Before this God we stand in awe, in wondering admiration. To this God we give our whole beings in worship.

"This is why you must know, and fix in your heart, that the Lord is God in the heavens above and on earth below, and that there is no other" (Dt 4:39). These are the words of Moses, telling the Israelites in the desert of the wonders that God performed "before your very eyes" (Dt 4:35), showing them his power in releasing them from Egypt, "by signs and wonders, by war, with his strong hand outstretched." This is the God that has been made known to us as the creator of heaven and earth, the "spirit, infinitely perfect," the judge of all men. For some, this is the God of fear.

St. Paul gives us an entirely different picture. We have been led by the "Spirit of God and are sons of God" (Rm 8:14). This is not a spirit of slavery, but a spirit of adoption, "through which we cry out, 'Abba' (that is, 'Father')" (Rm 8:15). The word "Abba" in its original understanding has a little deeper meaning than just the word "father." There is a connotation of endearment, not present in the word itself. The difference is subtle, but there just the same, much as the difference between "son," and "my son." This is the God of whom Jesus speaks, telling us to say "Our Father" when we pray, and calling him "your Father in heaven."

The beautiful part of it all is that these three aspects of God are in no way contradictory, but coalesce into the same image. God indeed is the awesome Trinity. God indeed is the creator and judge. But it is the same God who is our father. He is our father because he not so much created us as engendered us. He is our father because he engendered us out of love. And the beautiful thing about God's love is that it is as infinite and eternal as he is himself. It is not half-way, it is not fickle. Once God loves, that love is perfect and forever.

This is the God who has called us. We may have gotten the impression that God has called us for himself, to fulfill his own special purposes, to be sure that there were enough of us to go around, to spread his word to those who otherwise would be without it, to help keep his name alive in the world. These reasons are valid, but the primary reason why God has called us is for ourselves. His call is a further projection of his love for us. He places a demand on those he calls, as on Abraham. But he never fails to make his chosen ones aware of the gift that he intends to give. God loves us, and it is in his love for us that he calls us to special service. To this God, therefore, may we respond; to this God who promises us his peace; to this God who loves us; to this God who is truly our Father.

CHAPTER II
HERE, LORD, HERE I AM

There was a certain man from Ramathaim, Elkanah by name. He had two wives, one named Hannah, the other Peninnah. Peninnah had children, but Hannah was childless. This man went regularly on pilgrimage to worship the Lord of hosts and to sacrifice to him at Shiloh.

Hannah rose after one (of the sacrificial meals) at Shilo, and presented herself before the Lord. . . . In her bitterness, she prayed to the Lord, weeping copiously, and made a vow, promising: "O Lord of hosts, if you look with pity on the misery of your handmaid, if you remember me and not forget me, if you give your handmaid a male child, I will give him to the Lord for as long as he lives." When Elkanah had relations with his wife Hannah, the Lord remembered her. She conceived, and at the end of her term bore a son whom she called Samuel, since she had asked the Lord for him. . . . . Once he was weaned, she brought him up with her (to Shilo), along with a three year old bull, an ephah of flour, and a skin of wine and presented him at the temple of the Lord at Shilo. After the boy's father had sacrificed the young bull, Hannah, his mother, approached Eli and said: "Pardon, my Lord! As you live, my lord, I am the woman who stood near you here, praying to the Lord. I prayed for this child, and the Lord granted my request. Now I, in turn, give him to the Lord: as long as he lives, he shall be dedicated to the Lord" (1 Sm 1:1-3; 9-11; 19-20; 24-28).

The story of Hannah, the mother of Samuel, is one of the most beautiful in the whole of the bible. She had been childless, and back in those days, this was considered a mark of divine disfavor. Once each year, she went with her husband to offer sacrifice at the sanctuary at Shilo. On one occasion, while they were there she went before the Ark of the Lord, and filled with grief, she poured out her heart in prayer: "If you will send me a son, I will dedicate him to your service all of his life." As she prayed, she wept. Heli, the priest, saw her, and thinking that she had taken too much wine, reprimanded her. But she explained that she had been praying, earnestly seeking God's blessing. In the course of that year God heard her prayer, and blessed her with a son, Samuel. She waited until Samuel was three, before she returned to the sanctuary. She brought him to Heli, and said, "Do you remember me? This is the son I was praying for. I vowed him to the Lord. Here he is, take him."

Looking at the history of God's people in the Old Testament, we see that it is a perpetual swing between adversity and prosperity. Yet through it all, God seemed to provide himself with people of extraordinary devotion, like Hannah, who sometimes stood alone in times of unfaithfullness. But this is true of the history of the Church as well, right up to modern times. Pope Leo XIII was elected by the Cardinals merely as a "temporary" pope having left a sick bed to come to the conclave. He lived for twenty-five years, and his writings on modern social structures are as valid today as they were almost a hundred years ago when they were written. St. Pius X, at the beginning of our century, changed the whole thinking of the Church regarding Holy Communion, opening the way for both early and frequent Communion. Pope John the twenty-third was also elected at an age when most men have long retired, and proceeded to institute a change in the Church whose effects will be felt for years — centuries, maybe?

Today we see around us the violation of every basic human right, on every level, between persons, between people of different social levels and between nations. Yet we know, from the fact of divine providence, that evil never will overcome good. We are sure of this because, as we have seen, God has always provided himself with those special persons of exemplary virtue who have stood firm against the evils of the day. We may recall the story of Elijah, who complained that he was the only one in the whole of Israel who was faithful to Yahweh. He received the answer that Yahweh had reserved for himself five thousand men who had not yet bent their knees to Baal. Once again, for those special tasks, God has always provided himself with special people.

But God has a whole lot of ordinary tasks, as well. Whom does God call for these tasks? Just ordinary people, like you and me. And while the call to communicate Christ to others is "ordinary" in the sense that God speaks to us through others, the call can be considered a vocation in the true sense of the word.

Why has he chosen us and not others? Most simply, because all of us have more than just one such vocation. It is important, therefore, to remember that if God does call us to more than one, he gives us the talents to fulfill each.

How do we know that God is calling us? The most normal way for God to send us any kind of grace is

through others. We may see others whose lives are
enriched by their accepting such a call. We may be
encouraged to become involved by those in the religious
education program: priests, sisters and directors. We
may at times be asked directly. It may, however, be just
something inside us, some interior desire to do
something special, some unspoken wish — need,
almost — to give something of ourselves. There can be
no doubt that any or all of these are the manifestations
of God's call to us truly to share ourselves with others,
with our young people.

Perhaps if we examine the fact of providence itself,
this whole idea will become a little clearer. We
customarily think of providence as the simple fact of
God taking care of us, as he takes care of all his
creatures. We can surely recall the beautiful words of
Jesus himself who tells us that his father who provides
the birds with their food, and makes beautiful the
flowers, will certainly take care of all of our natural
needs. But if we stop here, what a limit we are putting
on the goodness and mercy of God! God's providence
towards us is synonymous with his love. And since the
love of God is directed towards our salvation,
providence means that at any given moment of our lives
God is present to us, giving us sufficient grace to live
with him in his own intimate life.

But providence is even more than this. It affects
every facet of our lives. Much of what we call
"coincidence" can be ascribed to the direct effect of the
action of God on us. Perhaps a personal experience can
illustrate this. Several years ago there was a young
couple who were coming to me for counselling. On this
one occasion, I was away on vacation visiting relatives.
It happened that the Thursday before first Friday came,
and a neighboring parish had need for another priest
for confessions. The temperature was well into the

nineties, and there I was, instead of relaxing with my family in some cool spot, cooking in my own juice in the confessional — the last place I wanted to be! But some time in the course of the evening, a person came in, and I was able to assist him. So far, so good. But when I returned to my own parish, I happened to meet this young couple, who told me they had come to see me, and finding me gone, talked to one of the other priests, "And he really helped us!" It has often struck me that this was no mere "coincidence." God put me in a place where I really should never have been at all, to help someone who needed it. And at the same time, took me away from the place where I did belong because he had someone else for a job which I wasn't able to do as well.

We may ask the question, "What would have happened if some of the people God called had said, 'No'?" Probably nothing as far as the plan of God is concerned, because his providence can make up for any human lack. But what a loss to the person himself! In the nineteenth chapter of the Gospel of St. Matthew (Mt 19:16 ff), we read the story of the "rich young man." He came with the question, "What must I do to attain eternal life?" Jesus told him, "Keep the commandments." He replied, "All these have I done since my youth." Now Jesus invites him to be "perfect" by selling all that he has and coming to follow him. Since the young man went away, refusing this perfect state, many interpret this action as the loss of everything, including his soul. But that need not be so. He would go on keeping the commandments, and so go on doing the things that would gain him eternal life. What he refused was Christ's special invitation, and what a refusal it was! Let us not forget that he went away "sad."

Who is to judge, however, the magnitude of the loss

of what possibly was an apostle to the souls of those to whom he may have administered? God's call to us is, to be sure, an invitation to serve him in a special way, to increase the kingdom of God on earth. More important- ly, it is an invitation to come closer to him, as was the invitation to the young man to be "perfect."

As an invitation, we are entirely free to accept or refuse. By refusing Christ's invitation, the young man in the Gospel did not totally reject God or his gifts, nor do we. But what a loss to ourselves! A loss in goodness, in service, in gratitude, in personal satisfaction, in the power to assist others.

There is no way of telling how many young people would be benefited by our acceptance, or what would be lost to them by our refusal. To accept the divine invitation, on the other hand, does require a great deal of faith and trust, as well as overcoming some pretty strong reasons for not accepting. Perhaps if we look at some of these reasons, we may be able to clarify our thinking, and find the power to be able to say with Abraham, "Here, Lord, here I am!"

Fear — insecurity — is first on the list. It takes a thousand nameless forms — contradictory forms — sometimes. We are not sure that it is God who is calling us. We are afraid that we are being presumptuous, that we are putting ourselves forward, that we are seeking to stand out among others. Conversely, we are afraid that we won't be accepted. Looking on all of this logically, it sounds kind of silly. But there is nothing silly about the turmoil that it causes us at the time. These fears may be undefinable, but they are there, and they make us hesitate.

Secondly, we wonder if we are going to have the time. We picture ourselves with armloads of books and materials, classes to prepare, homework to correct, projects to complete. We think about the fact that we will have to set aside a specific time each week for the actual teaching, and worry about whether we will be free to do it each week. Looking at this objection, we see that it really is a little selfish, but the thoughts are there, and they make us hesitate. We just don't want to "over-commit" ourselves.

The one objection that really disturbs us, though, is the thought of the magnitude of the task, and the responsibility that goes with it. The thought of all these young people who will depend upon us for Christian formation really makes us think twice. And it is not just the question of "teaching." We will come back to that. It is, instead, the question of communicating the whole of Christian living that really staggers us. These young people will look to us for this Christian living — to us, as models, as those who live the Christian life as well as preach it, as those who follow as well as lead, as those who seek goodness for ourselves as well as encourage it in others. Indeed, this is a task that seems beyond our capacities.

Then, can we teach? This one involves lots of things. Have we the knowledge sufficient to teach others? Much of the time, we feel that our own understanding of the truths of our faith is not as complete as it should be. So, knowing our own lack, we wonder if we can teach others. Secondly, can we teach, period? Have we the skills — and the patience — necessary to cope with all the "problems" that others tell us about? So much we don't know, so much we are unsure of, so much we have to learn — these are the things that trouble us. And again, these anxieties are real.

The last objection is of real concern to us. Somewhere along the line we realize that the task of bringing others close to Christ involves our own need to be close to him. In other words, we know that holiness is communicated, not taught. The only way we bring others to Christ is not by what we teach them, not by what we beat into them, even, but by *what we are.*

These are not neglible causes for hesitation. They are real. There are solutions to them, however. To begin with, if all of us waited until we "knew enough," the whole process of Christian education would be immobilized. None of us will ever get finished learning more and more about our Catholic faith. And positively, none of us will ever get finished striving for higher virtue, a greater awareness of the presence of God, a more perfect harmony with his will, a greater realization of his love.

Let us try to answer these difficulties in order. If we can recognize that it is God who is calling us, then may we place our full confidence in him. Personal fears and confidence in God are contradictories. If, therefore, there is a fault, it is the fact that we do not trust. It is an easy thing to talk about confidence, especially to someone else. We all know what the books say. We have heard time and again that God will take care of us and all our needs. What we really need is to apprehend this truth on the level of personal acceptance. To do this, we need only to set aside the "book truth" and take a look at our own lives in the past. Not one of us, if we take the time to consider, can be unaware of the goodness of God as he has manifested it to us personally. How many times has he made his presence almost physically felt; how many times has he given us the sense of having been forgiven for our offenses; how many times have we felt his peace. These are manifestations of the presence of God within us, a presence that frees from all fear.

Going back to the question. "Will we have the time?" Our first response to the interior call of God was correct. Yes. We need, it is true, a spirit of generosity. Considering, however, all that God has done for us, and reflecting on these graces, responding in generosity is not hard.

When we come to the question of our talents and ability, we are indeed in doubt. And again, it is simplistic in the extreme just to say that if God is calling us, he will provide us with the means to carry out his call. Just the same, there are two things we may consider. God has given us some talents, and we may count on these to fulfill the things required by the call. But most importantly, we ought not sell short the work of the Holy Spirit. This is something we have to experience, not something we can be told about. More times than we can number, we find ourselves with a thought, an idea, an inspiration, that just has to be divine in its origin. More times than we can count, this happens right when we are teaching. This does not mean, obviously that we can go without preparation, depending on the gift known as "dabitur vobis," that what to say will be given to us, but it does mean that the Holy Spirit provides a positive inspiration in our teaching as we are teaching. Why should we wonder at this? The whole thing comes from God; the purpose, the call, the process.

Can we teach? Actually, there are two considerations to be answered. The first is, what are the mechanics of teaching? Some very practical things go into this. First of all, we need to be familiar with the classroom, or the facility that we will have for teaching. Know where everything is, know what materials are available. Learning the actual process of teaching, however, involves a whole bundle of things. These are just a few suggestions.

Hopefully, your diocese or parish will have a teachers' training course. There is really no substitute for this, so obviously, enroll and learn. It is just that simple.

Prepare your classes well, and be prepared to spend some time on this preparation. For every hour's teaching, you may find yourself spending about four hours of preparation. Don't let this frighten you. It will be the most rewarding time of your life, not only giving you the assurance that you will know well what you must teach, but opening your own mind to an awareness of the truth that you never had before. In this process of preparation, one thing is absolutely essential. Use your teacher's manual, and certainly in the beginning, follow it faithfully. There is no substitute for this, either. A second thing will be extremely helpful. If there are more than one class of the grade you are teaching, try to prepare your lessons with the other teachers. You, who are new teachers will benefit tremendously from this — from the ideas, the experience, the know-how of the older teachers. But you will be able to contribute too and as you do, you will grow in confidence.

The second consideration is that indefinable quality that makes a "good" teacher, that separates a teacher from someone conducting a class. Can we be such a teacher? Father Charles Curran, in one of his lectures, has said that a teacher "is in pain to be understood." In other words, his desire to communicate is an intensity of fire burning within him. There is only one way that we can make this happen. To be on fire ourselves with the truth within us. To be so enflamed with the significance, the value, the magnificence of the truth that it becomes a real need to share it with our students. Teaching skills are important, but nothing like the importance of this desire that burns, a flame of fire within us!

Finally, we come to the question, "Are we good enough?" Will we be good enough example to the children? In short, are we holy enough? That's a good question; are there anymore questions? Nobody really knows the answer. When we read the autobiographies of some of the real saints in the Church, we are struck by the consistency of this point of self-appraisal: they felt themselves to be the most miserable of sinners. We have a tendency to say, "How can this be?" They were the greatest of saints! If we look at holiness, not as a state, but as a process, the answer is really simple. They saw themselves at any given moment in the process of becoming holy, not where they were, but where they ought to have been. More than anything, however, they had a keen awareness of the fact that the call to holiness was a gift from God, and that the fault was their own lack of cooperation with that gift.

Perhaps we aren't holy enough to have this concept of ourselves. Considering again, however, that holiness is a process, we may at least consciously tend towards it. We will have more to say about holiness in a later chapter, but for a quick definition, this will suffice: holiness is the growing conscious awareness of the presence of God in our lives, and the growing response to that presence by our striving to do what he wants. Truly, we are not saints — yet! We do have to be willing to grow along spiritual lines.

There is one final consideration. That is gratitude to God for all these gifts that he has given to us. St. Paul, in the letter to the Corinthians, places teaching among the charismatic gifts. It is essential to remember that these are gifts given to the individual, not necessarily to build him up, but precisely for the building up of the Church. In other words, it is a gift to be given in turn to others. But we need not look upon this as something special. This is the ordinary way that God does things. He uses us in the completion of his divine plan. The whole of salvation history is a demonstration of this. So are our lives. So true is this that we may say that God never gives us a grace just for ourselves. A moment's thought will convince us. Practically every spiritual value, including faith itself, in our lives has come to us from some other person. In other words, God has used others to communicate grace to us on every level. He expects us to continue these graces by communicating them to others.

Summing it all up, all of us started at one time or another. We all felt our inadequacies, some of us, rather keenly. Further, we will never be finished learning more and more about our faith, understanding it more deeply, or living it more perfectly, and in greater holiness. We will never, moreover, get finished, through knowledge and experience, seeking to become better as teachers. There is one thing, however, that we may all, beginners or veterans, bring to our students. And of all the things we bring them, this is the one necessary and most lasting — a personal interest in each individual, or better, some gift, some share of ourselves.

I will never forget my own fourth grade teacher. She was a lay person, and she had that special quality — a real charisma — of making each one of us feel we were important. She never did succeed in improving my handwriting, or cure me of the habit of saying "ain't," but of the many people who have influenced my life, I see her as one who has affected it most positively. I am sure she has contributed a great deal to my own vocation. I still see one or another of my former classmates, and we still talk about her. She is dead now, but then again, she isn't! She still lives — in all of us. This is what we may bring to our students.

In summary, it is God who has called us, and it is God who has given us the talents to accept that call. We do need confidence, and perhaps a great deal of it, but that confidence is not unfounded when we place it entirely in God. We need a spirit of willingness, and a spirit of generosity. These can be a response in gratitude to all that God has given us. Conscious of our continuing needs, but equally conscious that it is God who is calling, God who will fulfill those needs, may we say, "Here, Lord, here I am!"

CHAPTER III
TO WHAT ARE WE CALLED?

Now this is how the birth of Jesus Christ came about. When his mother MARY was engaged to Joseph, but before they lived together, she was found with child through the power of the Holy Spirit. Joseph, her husband, an upright man unwilling to expose her to the law, decided to divorce her quietly. Such was his intention when suddenly an angel of the Lord appeared in a dream and said to him: "Joseph, son of David, have no fear about taking Mary as your wife. It is by the Holy Spirit that she has conceived this child. She is to have a son and you are to name him Jesus because he will save his people from their sins."

When Joseph awoke, he did as the angel of the Lord had directed him and received her into his home as his wife. He had no relations with her at any time before she bore a son, whom he named Jesus.

After they (the astrologers) had left, the angel of the Lord suddenly appeared in a dream to Joseph with the command: "Get up, take the child and his mother, and flee to Egypt. Herod is searching for the child to destroy him." Joseph got up and took the child and his mother and left that night for Egypt. He stayed there until the death of Herod (Mt 1:18-21; 24-25; 13-15).

St. Joseph had all the qualities of a man truly devoted to God. His obedience to the divine will, of course, stands out among them as the traditional light in the darkness or city upon a hill. We may recall that his obedience was immediate, without comment, perfectly carried out. Along with that, there was a total trust in God. These two qualities are manifested in the Gospel story (Mt 1). The angel appeared to him and told him not to be afraid to take Mary as his wife. So, "when Joseph awoke, he did as the angel told him." Later, the angel warned him about Herod, so again, "Joseph got up, took the child and his mother, and left that night for Egypt." If St. Joseph is the model of anything, he surely is the model of simple acceptance of the will of God.

Every Christian, by the very fact of his call to faith in Christ, has the vocation to holiness. Holiness, therefore, far from being the exclusive property of candidates for canonization, is for all, and according to the measure of divine grace given to each, is attainable by all. The Fathers of the Vatican Council, in Chapter Five of the Dogmatic Constitution of the Church (no. 39), are emphatic about this. They tell us that "all in the Church, whether they belong to the hierarchy or are cared for by it, are called to holiness. This holiness of the Church is constantly shown forth in the fruits of grace which the spirit produces in the faithful and so it must be; it is expressed in many ways by the individuals, who, each in his own state of life, tend to the perfection of love, thus sanctifying others." We believe that we have been called to this holiness, not just as the ordinary Christian, but in a special way, as teachers, specifically sent to bring Christ to others.

It is a call, moreover, that demands an acceptance as complete as St. Joseph's, with all the burdens, sacrifices, and joys that go with it. Above all else, it is a call not just for others, but for ourselves. It is a call to personal holiness. Most of us are afraid of the word holiness, or sanctity. As far as we are concerned, holiness is for saints. We look upon them as persons especially called to heroic virtue by God himself, and who have responded perfectly to his call. While essentially this is true, there is a level of holiness attainable by all, a level that God desires for all.

What is personal holiness? There are undoubtedly as many definitions of it as there are persons to define it. If we look into the lives of the saints, however, we find a common thread, a common denominator. In all of them, there was an overpowering sense of the presence of God. This is true of the saints of the Old Testament; Abraham, for example, who walked with God; David, who relied on God through his flight from Saul and from Absolom; Jeremiah, in whom the word of God burned like a fire. This is true of our Christian saints, as well: St. Joseph, the model of acceptance; St. Ignatius of Antioch, who knew that Christ would be with him as he faced the lions in Rome; St. Catherine of Siena, who built a little chapel in her heart, where she retired in prayer in the midst of a busy day; St. Therese, who gave to Jesus all the "little things" of her life as sacrifices to him.

The fact of the divine presence is, certainly, the first requisite in the definition of holiness. The awareness of it, to be sure, is an indefinable thing, but a real thing just the same. It is something we feel or perhaps, when it is not there, something we "don't feel," much like the sense of aloneness that comes to us when nobody else is home. And yet, when it is there, we may be completely calm, we may face any difficulty, we may be free from all fear, we may answer any call. We would like this sense of the divine presence to remain with us, but unfortunately it does not. It really is a gift, as so many other divine things are. The best we can do is to be open to it, to rejoice in it, to keep alive the memory of it.

Along with the sense of divine presence, the saints manifested a marvelous confidence in God. Jeremiah, in the maelstrom of violent personal persecution, was held together by the promise that God would be with him. St. Ignatius faced the lions of Rome, sure in his confidence that he would not be alone. In the difficulties of our own life, we see the need of confidence, we pray for it, we are encouraged by others to "trust in God." The easiest thing we ourselves do is to tell others likewise to trust in God, but where does this trust come from?

Perhaps a more fundamental question is, "Just what is confidence in God?" It builds on the sense of divine presence, adding to it the fact of God's infinite goodness, his infinite love. Here we run into a kind of split. We know, from what we have heard about God — the external input, so to speak — that he created us out of love. And once God does something, because he is totally without change, he is committed to that act eternally. So that, if God has loved me at all, he must love me still. This we may believe, because it is a theological fact. In the language of the philosophers, it is metaphysically true, in no way can it be untrue. Like everything else in our spiritual life, however, there is a vast chasm between theological truth and personal acceptance.

Confidence in God must be experienced. Looking at others, even the saints, does not help much. If we look back into our own lives, however, we can see that we have experienced it. All we need to do is to recall the many instances — or even a single instance — when we were praying for something "special," something we really felt we needed, in fact, we had to have. Recall that God seemed to have said "No." Recall that only later, and sometimes, much later, we discovered that by this apparent refusal, God gave a greater gift. Through it all, we may have even wondered "What ever happened to all those prayers?" Nothing. Nothing at all. God just answered the "wrong" prayer. He may not have given us what we asked for, but what we should have asked for. We have every reason, therefore, just from our own experience, to begin, at least, to trust in God.

Returning to our definition of holiness as manifested in the lives of saints, another quality that we note is humility. We are all aware of the fact that humility does not mean grovelling around on the ground, calling ourselves the most miserable of sinners. It certainly does not mean false humility, as if Nadia Comaneci were to say, "I am not a very good gymnast." She just happens to be the best in the world at the moment! Thirty-five years ago, the priest who gave us our retreat in preparation for ordination, Father Joseph Schaggemann, defined humilty, and the definition is still valid. He said that humility is an honest appraisal of ourselves before God, before others, and towards ourselves. Before God, it is total reliance; before others, it is condescension, meaning to come down to their level; and towards ourselves, it is self-acceptance, this is who we are. Perhaps it is just the quality of knowing our limitations, of never taking ourselves too seriously. This is why saints always thought of themselves as "miserable sinners." They saw themselves not as we see them now, actively seeking to live as God would have them, but in their failure to cooperate with the grace that God had bestowed on them. Holiness is indeed a gift. And the closer we attain to true holiness, the more we realize that we are not so much giving as being given. It is with a deep sense of gratitude and a deep sense of unworthiness that we may accept this call to holiness.

We have already said much about conformity to the
will of God as essential to accepting his call. It has to be,
certainly, the hub of the whole thing. When we look at
the saints, we see conformity beyond anything we know
we can accomplish. Saint Therese, calling herself a
"little saint," sought to accept everything in her life for
the love of Jesus, paying attention to the little things
particularly, because she felt that she should not
accomplish "big things." In her autobiography, she
tells how she tried to do this. Right off the top of our
heads, we might think that this is comparatively easy,
but just try it sometime! Try just staying calm — even
for the love of God — in the hundred and one
exasperating little things that turn up in our lives just
for one day! We may get a better picture of conformity to
God's will from this, seeing conformity not as simple
"acceptance," but as an active desire to please.

Don't jump off the bridge yet! Help is on the way!
Let's go back to the fact that the whole thing comes
from God first, that holiness, in its basic definition, is a
gift from him. He gave that gift in an extraordinary
measure to the saints. To what degree he will give it to
us is entirely up to him, and his purpose for us. What is
certain, is that we already have some degree of personal
holiness. What is equally certain is that he will
continue to endow us with it, and increase it in us.

We come now to the manner in which God brings
this holiness about. He could, of course, just make us
holy, and in a sense, he does that. There are special
spiritual forces, however, that he puts into our lives that
bring holiness about, each of them working in us in
their own distinctive way.

The beginning, the foundation of all is the gift we
call *sanctifying grace*. There are many definitions of
sanctifying grace, and in the last few years, many new
ones. The one that seems to make the most sense, and

the one that most exactly describes what it does in our souls, is to say that *sanctifying grace* is the life of God in us. We call it, therefore, supernatural life. This indeed, tells us both the nature and the function of this gift. It is an abiding, lasting, permanent state of existence, rather than something that we put on, as a coat. By the very fact that it is life, it gives us the power to perform supernatural actions. We look at all living things, we see that it is the fact of life itself that gives them the power of "interior self-action." Supernaturally, it is the same. We have come alive in God. By that very gift of life itself, we have the power to live for him, to act for him. The life of God itself is our supernatural "interior self-action," whereby all our actions are turned toward him. *Sanctifying grace*, therefore, is the foundation and the beginning of all supernatural life and action.

We have other natural powers in addition to natural life, and so we have other supernatural powers in addition to grace. These, as is grace itself, are infused by God. We might call them the package of supernatural action. Briefly, these are the infused virtues, actual graces, the gifts of the Holy Spirit, and special divine inspirations.

First among these infused supernatural powers, are the three divine virtues, faith, hope and love. In what way are they powers? All of us have certain natural talents, talents that give us a liking for certain actions or skills, and a real ease in doing them. There are people with a talent for music, for example, whose ability to perform astounds us. Without a doubt, this power is a special gift. In contrast, therefore, to the general understanding of virtue as something acquired, the infused virtues are supernatural talents in a similar way as are natural talents. Very simply, they are given us by God. And for the same reason, to make our supernatural actions pleasant and easy.

A second point about the divine virtues is that they
lead us directly to God. This in fact, is the reason they
are called divine or theological. Thus, by faith, in
contrast to believing simply "all that God has taught,"
we believe in God himself. We have already touched on
the fact of faith as coming from God, but we can review
it here as a part of our consideration of these virtues.
While faith leads us to God, the beginning of faith, as
we have said, comes to us from the outside, from others.
We believe those who have told us about God. At some
special time in our lives, possibly in our teens, we have
to face a challenge. Most often, it is the choice of good
over evil, over sin. We recognized this as a call from God
himself, a call, moreover, that is forceful and positive.
Most importantly, it is a call to please God. Now we
have made an act of faith in God, a personal being, who
has called us from within ourselves, whom we have
chosen to please.

This call leads us to three distinct acts of faith.
Number one, God is. God is, not just a natural force,
not just a supreme power and intelligence, not just a
"spirit, infinitely perfect," but a "person," someone
who knows us. The second truth is, God is my creator.
We are not biological accidents, we have been made by
God himself, by a direct act of his will. For this reason,
there is a relationship between us, a relationship of
concern on his part, a relationship of dependence on
ours. Finally, God is my Creator who has made me out
of love. There are all kinds of testimonies — Sacred
Scripture is loaded with them — of God's love for us.
My own personal awareness of the love of God for me
comes from these two things: theologically, all his acts
proceed from his love, because in him there is no
possibility of evil; he has given me the power, the
freedom to love. Thus, faith goes far beyond the
formula, "I believe in God," and truly brings us to God

himself, God to whom we may relate personally, God in whom we see the source of all goodness, God who loves us.

God, in whom we see the source of all goodness, is the object of the virtue of hope. We use the word "hope" to signify this virtue, but in our present usage, the word has a different connotation. We "hope" it does not rain, or that our students understand the lesson, but these are no more than fervent wishes. The virtue of hope, on the other hand, is confidence, confidence that the goodness of God will conquer all things, and ultimately give us the grace to attain eternal life. A better term, therefore, in our usage, would be "trust." Sometimes we hear that the motive for this trust is God's power, or even his fidelity. But really, it is the same God of goodness and love who is the object of our faith who is likewise the object of our trust. We who have experienced this goodness and love have only to keep it in mind to be sure that it will always be a part of our lives, even when things seem to be going badly.

Through the virtue of trust, we have confidence that God will give us eternal life. This is reflected in just about all the prayers of the Church, especially those at Mass. Heaven, however, is not the only object of the virtue. We can have it for this life as well. One of the greatest of all gifts from God himself is the capacity to see his goodness and love in all the things that transpire in our lives, good and bad, joyful and sorrowful, easy and hard to live with. Too many people get attached to the idea of a "vale of tears," as if God put us here just to suffer. He put us here to live, but to live full of confidence in him. Trust sees God, therefore, as the source of all good and only good: *all good*, the ultimate cause of everything worthwhile that takes place in our lives, whether it seems that way or not; *only good* — and here we come to one of those metaphysical things — it is against his nature for him to intend evil. Trust in God is one of the beautiful virtues, guaranteed to free us from all anxiety, all worry, and bringing us the peace we all talk about. For us who are taking on the immense task of bringing Christ to others, it is a most necessary virtue. It gives us the power to be confident that we will have the grace of God working in us and through us.

When we first read in St. Thomas that the virtue of trust is related to the first beatitude, "How blest are the poor in spirit, the reign of God is theirs" (Mt 5:3), we think that it is difficult to understand. If, however, we see poverty of spirit as a realization of total spiritual need, we can begin to comprehend the relationship. It is, indeed, just another way of saying that by ourselves we have no capacity to accomplish anything of spiritual value, but that God who is all powerful can do all things, even through us. Our prayer could readily be,"Free us from the notion that we are anything without You."

"Love, love, love," is the catchword of today. How differently, however, do we understand the infused virtue of love from the many meanings of the word in present usage. The virtue is the divine gift enabling us to return God's own love to him, and through him to show love to others. In the modern use of the word, it can mean things as divergent as self-sacrifice and passion. It is too bad that a word with such a truly deep, beautiful, real meaning as this one should be so indifferently used as to alter the beauty of its connotation. If we are to understand the meaning of the virtue, however, we may begin with the definition of love from the first letter of St. John, "God is love" (1 Jn 4:9). God is love. God, therefore, does not just have love, or just show love, but God *is* love. God is the perfect personification of infinite love. (All human love, therefore, the more perfectly it is modeled after the love of God, the more perfect it is). If we think for a moment, we see that there is nothing material, nothing human, nothing physical about God's love, for the simple reason that he does not have any body. His love is entirely spiritual. Because, moreover, he is infinitely perfect, he is in need of nothing, so he loves only to give. When we total all this up, we come to one conclusion: the love of God, in its essence and in its act, is the total outpouring of God himself to his rational creatures, man and angels.

We have experienced this love, in the sense that we have experienced the gift of God himself. Our life is a share in God's own life, our supernatural life is a share in the power to live with him, our faith is the interior awareness of his very presence within us. Above all, however, our capacity for freedom is a share in God's own power to love. This gift of freedom, of all the gifts he has given us, has to be one of the greatest. We generally think of freedom as the power of choice. Actually, it is the power to love. The very essence of love is free act. For this reason no one can force us to love. One can make us want to love, as it were, by showing us such goodness that we wish to return it, but no one can make us *love*. To love another is an act that must come entirely from within us. To be able to love is God's greatest gift. He creates us in full freedom, including the full freedom to reject his love, as well as the freedom to love in return. This is the gift, this is the virtue, to share not just in the love of God, but in the infinite freedom of God.

Obviously, to love in such superabundance as this, we ought to respond. This we do with gratitude. With marvelous logic, the words for both *gift* and *thanks* have the same root, *charis* in Greek, and *gratia* in Latin. With marvelous logic, we say, because as a gift is something freely given, so also is gratitude something freely given. With gratitude, therefore, may our love of God begin. We need not here re-enumerate all the gifts of God; we may just recall his gifts of spirit, life, grace, freedom, and all the personal blessings we have experienced. Since every gift of God is an outpouring of his love, we seek to return this giving in gratitude by some gift of ourselves. At what point in this process, gratitude becomes love in its purest sense, is a question we may never be able to answer. What is essential is that the return comes from within ourselves, freely.

As divine virtues, therefore, faith, hope and love are the God given powers to believe, trust and love him, but to do so in a way that God is made real in us. This real presence is a source of satisfaction, or joy. We may go still farther in our consideration of faith, confidence and love. St. Paul lists these three among the charismatic gifts. Reading the twelfth, thirteenth and fourteenth chapters of his first letter to the Corinthians, we are struck with this insistence that God is working in his people in a special way, to instruct, to admonish, to increase their spiritual powers. From this insistence, we learn the basic characteristic of the charismatic gifts — some special outward sign of God in us, not for us, but for the "building up of the Church" (14,19).

Faith as a charismatic gift goes well beyond the simple phrase, "I believe in God," goes beyond the response to the virtue of accepting God in our hearts, and even goes beyond that deep conviction of the presence of God in us. All of these need be no more than interior acts, affecting only ourselves. As we have said, charismatic gifts are given rather for others. Thus, the faith that is a gift has the quality of standing out from us, a true "light shining before man" (Mt 5,16), a certain something in us that is easily recognized by others, whereby they look inside themselves, and are inspired to a more perfect faith. It is not, on the other hand, the "pushy" kind of thing, that constant reminding everyone "put your trust in God." It is instead, a quiet thing, a calm, simple awareness of God's presence that others just know is there.

Margaret had just this kind of faith. She was comparatively young — in her forties — but a severe heart condition kept her at home. She had a deep faith in the presence of our Lord in the Blessed Sacrament, and a deep faith in God and his goodness, even in her sickness. She never, for example, spoke of "Holy Communion." when the priest came, but always said, simply "Jesus." As her condition grew worse, there was only one hope for survival, and that was open heart surgery. It took a special kind of courage to undergo this one. The doctor told her that if the operation were successful, she would be a completely well woman. But if it weren't, she would not live through it. With that marvelous strength of faith, she told me, the evening before the surgery, "God is good to me. I really have nothing to lose. If the doctor is successful, I shall be well again, to take care of my family. If he isn't, tomorrow, at this time I shall be in heaven." That tomorrow, she was in heaven. But she still lives, in all of us, in her faith.

St. Paul, in First Corinthians, mentions trust among the charismatic gifts, along with faith and love, and surely there is room for it. There are people whose trust in God is so firm that they are able to stand against all fear, so calm that they are free from all anxiety, so beautiful that we admire it in wonder, so other-worldly that we are sure that it is a special gift. It is such a gift, with implications so deep, that it not only transforms the person, but cannot fail to affect all of us who are inspired by it.

Ken, a recovering alcoholic, lives with such a gift. He recently suffered his fourth heart attack, and was truly near death. Most people who go through such an experience say later that it is devastating. First of all, there is intense pain. Most importantly, however, they suffer great fear and mental turmoil, and who can blame them. Ken was brought into the emergency room of the local hospital in a state of total calm, as outwardly unperturbed as if he had merely sprained his ankle. He nearly "blew the minds" of everybody there, including the doctor. They had never seen anyone this calm, in this serious condition. He told me about it later. "While they were bringing me to the hospital, I just said, 'God, if you want me, I'm ready. If you don't, that's all right, too.' " Such an attitude just has to be a gift, a gift that first of all blesses indeed the one who has it, but blesses us too, who see it, and are inspired by it.

Love is one of the three divine virtues. It is also, very definitely, one of the charismatic gifts. In the thirteenth chapter of First Corinthians, St. Paul presents a panegyric of love. Most of us, as we read this chapter, just sit back and sort of admire, knowing we will never have this kind of love, and wondering, in fact, if there is anyone who will ever have. If, however, we see love as a charismatic gift, then we begin to understand it as given by God to certain special, selected souls, for the "building up of the Church." We understand, also, the need for love, as heroic as this: "patient, not jealous, not putting on airs; never rude, not self-seeking, not brooding over injuries" (1 Cor 13:4-6).

St. Paul says, (1 Cor 12:31, 13:1) "set your hearts on the greater gifts. I will show you a way that surpasses all others." Anyone who has been given this charismatic gift of love has indeed been blessed by God. It is, however, the kind of gift we cannot let go of once we have it. Through it we make a committment to loving others that is totally unselfish, totally self-giving. Sometimes we may wonder if we are capable of loving to this degree. On the other hand, let us not think that this kind of love is only for those who have been given the gift. We may do more than just sit back and admire the gift and those who have it. We may see it as an ideal, and as all ideals, valid and attainable. It takes, however, a little courage, a little confidence, a little willingness to want to attain it. With these, we may be able to "set our hearts on the greater gifts," and seek — and pray for — the one that "surpasses all others."

Talents, however great they be, all by themselves, are not enough. How often we hear of a rather good musician "who never had a lesson." Sounds great, but how much better would he be if he had a few! In other words, talents must be brought to fruition by some additional power. Supernaturally, this power is actual grace. Really we should speak of "actual graces," because in the providence of God, these helps are manifold and repeated. Without a doubt, some of them are strictly interior. Most, however, come to us from the outside.

Not often, but on occasion, in time of prayer, I feel myself touched by God, in so far as he opens my mind to some spiritual insight, perhaps one that I have been seeking. Most of the time, it is just a better understanding of myself, in answer to one of my immediate spiritual needs. The experience, however, coming as it does at just that precise time, is undoubtedly the communication of God himself. It is positive. It is real.

I have already related the experience of God using my absence from the parish to bring about his own purpose. This is just one of the many and I have to say, growing number of "coincidences" which have no other real explanation than the providence of God in action. While this is so, actual graces, most of which come to us from others, are a part of the ordinary providence of God. These are the upbringing in a good

Christian home, the influence of really good people in our lives, the opportunity of a Christian education, among many others. The important thing about all of these actual graces, is that they bring to fruition the God-given talents, and as such are gifts from God.

In addition to this first set of supernatural powers, God gives us a second set, a parallel set, actually. These consist in the gifts of the Holy Spirit, made active by certain special divine inspirations. Why a second set? We may say that the gifts are "supercharged" supernatural talents, supercharged virtues. Whereas, the virtues assist us to do what is good, the gifts assist us to perform it more readily.

Many think of the "Gifts of the Holy Spirit" as given to us at Confirmation. Actually, they are given to us any time we receive the gift of sanctifying grace. They are a part of the spiritual package of powers given us by God to live close to him, and to act in a way that we tend toward him. But just what are they, and what are they for?

We have already called them "supercharged supernatural talents." One might say that they represent the difference between talent and genius. Once again, the virtues, activated by actual graces, enable us to do the ordinary things, pleasing to God. As we have pointed out, these virtues and actual graces are absolutely necessary if we are to do good at all. It is a doctrine of the Church that no one can avoid sin perpetually without the help of divine grace. But we, as Christians, are called to more than just goodness, we are called to holiness. Since we are called to communicate this same Christian living to others, the need for holiness is doubled. Thus, while these gifts are given to every one endowed with the gift of grace, they become important factors in our search for holiness. These gifts, by giving us a kind of "connaturality" in performing supernatural actions, not only make them easy, but make them pleasurable, enjoyable. Endowed with the Gifts, therefore, we are drawn to virtuous acts, to goodness, to God; drawn, moreover, with ease, with joy, with satisfaction.

St. Thomas, in his *Summa Theologica*, tells us the special function of each of these Gifts. Wisdom is the power to make a correct judgment concerning divine things, and to regulate our lives according to divine rules. To put it more simply, we may say that wisdom is the gift that enables us to see all things in the eyes of God. This may sound like a simple thing to do, but is it? It means the capacity to look through the apparent values of material or human things to the real values of divine things. It means the capacity to look beyond immediate results of our own actions to the results of what we do. It means the capacity to watch our own plans fail, with the sure knowledge that our failure contributes to the overall success of the divine plan. Applying this to our teaching of religion, it means that the failure of this particular project, or even with this particular child, need not mean that God is not with us. The gift of wisdom gives us the power to see through all of this to know that the power and grace of God — not ourselves — can and will bring about its own goodness, in spite of our personal failures, sometimes even because of them.

No wonder that wisdom is equated with both the love of charity, and with peace. It takes a special kind of love to be able to see the love of God in our lives when we seem to be "wiped out." It brings about a special kind of peace to be able, in the midst of some personal distress, to see beyond our own plans to the wonderful, loving plan of God.

The distinction between the gift of understanding and the gift of knowledge seems to be rather subtle. What we have to do, therefore, is to take the meaning of the words themselves. To know simply means to grasp the truth as such, the facts, as it were. To understand means to penetrate into the hidden meaning of these same things, this same truth. To illustrate, I know that there are three persons in one God, but to understand the meaning of the Trinity, even in an obscure way, is something else. We must remember, however, that these are gifts of the Holy Spirit, and therefore, special spiritual powers with which we have been endowed.

Knowledge is surely a part of faith. And since faith leads us directly to God himself, so does the gift of knowledge. It might be hard to see the distinction between the virtue of faith, whereby our minds are opened to the vision of God, and the gift of knowledge. The Gifts, we have said, are "supercharged" virtues, and for that reason, increase their powers. The gift of knowledge increases faith not by opening our minds to *more* revealed truths, but by giving us the power to believe more firmly whatever God has revealed. Faith enables us to see God; knowledge enables us to see him more clearly.

Understanding also adds to faith, but in a different way. Whereas knowledge enables us to believe more strongly, understanding enables us to believe with greater comprehension. Thus, by faith and knowledge we possess strong conviction in the Real Presence of Jesus in the Blessed Sacrament. By the gift of understanding we see the many facets of this truth, the many ways Jesus' presence relates to us. For example, his presence means the renewal of his sacrifice, his abiding presence in the Sacrament, our sharing in his divine life as we receive him.

The other gifts have the same relationship to some of the other virtues. The gift of counsel adds the depth of divine assistance to the virtue of prudence. By this gift we are able to know more surely the right thing to do in all matters of conduct, not only in the difference between right and sin, but especially in the difference between the perfect and the good.

The Gift of fortitude strengthens the virtue of fortitude. We often hear fortitude is the special gift of the martyrs. There is absolutely no question about that, that these were gifted with a super amount of it. But all of us are in sad shape if martyrs are the only ones who possess it. In our modern world, the Christian has the absolute need of the gift as well as the virtue of fortitude. Take the example of a salesman on an expense account. He tries to be honest in reporting his legitimate business expenses to the company. Because of this, the amount he reports is consistently lower than that of the others. They get together and tell him in plain English "he had better" pad his expenses or they will make it difficult for him. To stand up against this kind of pressure requires a special kind of fortitude, a special gift from God.

The gifts we call piety and fear of the Lord are like two sides of the same coin. Actually, in the book of Isaiah (11: 2-3), the same word is used. Through the gift of fear, we see the infinite perfection of God, and reverence his holiness. Through the gift of piety, this reverence gives way to wonder, that the God of infinite perfection should love us as children.

As the virtues are made operative by the actual graces that God sends us, so are the gifts made operative by special divine inspirations. These inspirations, superior to actual graces, are entirely interior. God opens his mind to us, revealing his special will for us, calling us to perfection. We experience through these inspirations a constant growth in personal insight. When do they come to us? Anytime, actually, but most often at time of quiet prayer. We find ourselves in close communication with God, when suddenly — and it is sudden — God speaks to us in some intimate way. We have to be ready, we have to be open, and have to be willing.

All of these things work to bring about holiness, holiness as coming from God, as a gift from him. Essentially, "this is where it's at." God, however, does not just pour holiness into us as we pour gas into our tank. We have to be receptive, and the more receptive, the greater the measure that we receive. Receptiveness takes many forms, but among these forms, we may distinguish four acts.

First, we have to know who we are. Today, in some psychologies of spirituality, the professed need is for a "good" self-image. Far more importantly, is a — or perhaps "the" — correct image. To attain this, we need to make an honest self-appraisal. The question we ask ourselves is not, "Who do I think I am?", but "Who am I really?" The reason for this is that self deception is without a doubt the greatest hindrance to spiritual progress. As long as we are blind to our faults, as long as we think ourselves more virtuous than we really are, as long as we see no real need to improve, then we are going to remain spiritually inactive. This could be spiritually fatal, because the spiritual life, as all kind of life, must continue to grow, otherwise it will debilitate, and eventually die.

The struggle for self-honesty is, therefore, a constant thing, and it is anything but easy. We begin with our motives. Try this one for openers. "Am I really trying to please God even in the good things I do for others, or am I really seeking some personal approval?" Or this one, "Do I really want to be free of some fault, such as impatience?" Sometimes we are surprised when we face such questions honestly, perhaps for the reason that we never did it before in just this way. But it is worth the struggle, because it opens us to ourselves in our inmost selves, it gives us the opportunity to see "who we really are."

Self knowledge is important, but it is only the first act. A second form of receptiveness, self acceptance, is equally important. I must accept full responsibility, not just for my actions, but for me, the person. The difference may be subtle, but it is real. If I just look at my actions, I can easily squirm out of any blame. I can make all sorts of phony excuses: "I didn't mean it; I wasn't thinking; the Devil made me do it." If, however, I take the focus off my actions and put it where it belongs, on me, I have to face the fact: I am responsible. I freely made myself who I really am.

One thing we must remember. The whole process of attaining holiness comes from God himself, and therefore, depends entirely on him. A major part of this whole process is to accept the fact that we are incapable of making any spiritual progress by ourselves. To reduce this to its logical conclusion, however, could lead us to a massive state of discouragement. We free ourselves from this with the confidence that God can and will assist us. The thought that comes to us might be this, "I have no power to enable me to grow spiritually, but God does." Anybody can have this thought, or even say it in the form of a prayer. But to accept this on the deep level of feeling, on the level of true conviction, sometimes requires what we may call a spiritual experience. This can come in a variety of ways, but the best way to describe it — if we can even use that word — is to say that somewhere along in our struggle, God simply opens our minds and hearts to the reality of his presence, his power, his grace, his love. Then we know, with a knowledge born of God himself, that if he will, he can make us free.

The third act is prayer. How do you really pray? Perhaps it is not so much a question of "knowing how," as being willing to try. Prayer is really the simplest thing we do. We just have to place ourselves in a state of communication with God. We can do this in any number of ways. We may use set prayers, speak to God in our own words, meditate, or just be conscious of his presence. If, however, we are to respond to God's call to holiness, certainly we must take the time to pray. It is as simple as that.

The fourth act is service. God's call to holiness is primarily for ourselves. But remember, God never calls us to anything *just* for ourselves.His gifts are given to us to be shared with others. For this reason, our response to the call to holiness involves our willingness to serve. In this we have no less a model than Jesus himself, who says (Mt 20:28), "The Son of man has come not to be served, but to serve." There are all kinds of ways in which we may put this need to serve into operation. Perhaps we can cut through the whole maze of possible actions to come to one idea that rather neatly sums it all up. My mother had a word for it. Whenever we kids — there were six of us — would get into some selfish situation, she would say, "Have a little consideration for each other." Have a little consideration. Think about the other. See his need of the moment. If there is one single thing that we will always find hard to do, it is to take our attention from ourselves, and see the other person, see his need. This could be a little easier, perhaps, if we could begin to see Christ in them.

Let's pause here for a little recapitulation. Here we are Christians, endowed with the gift of divine life, by which we not only live in God, but are enabled to respond to him in a supernatural way. We have been endowed with special talents, the virtues, whereby all our actions tending us to God are made easy and joyful. We have been the recipients of God's special care through his providence, and his special helps to be close to him. We have been "supercharged" with Gifts of the Holy Spirit, made effective with intimate divine inspirations. Where has all of this led us?

One would imagine that someone who lives constantly under the influence of grace and the gifts of the Holy Spirit would show this in his actions. This is precisely what the fruits of the Holy Spirit are, the actions produced in us by the inspiration. They are these, traditionally: love, joy, peace, patience, benignity, goodness, long-suffering, mildness, faith, modesty, continency, chastity. We can divide them into three categories.

The first is our actions in response to influence outside us, people and things that put pressure on us. With patience, long-suffering, mildness, we put up with the things we cannot change, and that includes the people we cannot change. Next, we accept, live with, overcome the pressures — the temptations — inside ourselves. Here by modesty, continence, and chastity, we attain that beautiful self-control that so markedly points to the person of virtue, and brings us that interior and exterior calm. Finally, we establish a wonderful relationship with others. The acts of love spoken of here as the fruits, are those acts of love, that goodness, that kindness, that is no more than the outpouring of our desire to help others. There is a joy in this kind of goodness, a joy, in the manner of mercy, that blesses both him who gives and him who receives. And there is a peace, if for no other reason than that there is no cause for contention, no room for contention where there is love and joy.

We have said much about the qualities of holiness as they effect us interiorly, as they are truly within us. These fruits of the Holy Spirit are the qualities that others see in us. But of all the qualities of holiness that are manifested to the outside, there are two especially that mark it as the genuine article, as surely as a mint mark authenticates a coin, or the word "sterling" on silver.

Joy is first. Happiness and holiness go extraordinarily well together. The happiest people in existence right now are at the same time the holiest — and the opposite is also true. These are they who live with God in heaven. One cannot get there unless he is holy — and the whole purpose is to be happy. There is, therefore, no such thing as a sad saint. So true is this that if you would find a sad "saint," believe this, you have not found a saint. The reason is simple. Holiness is essentially a call from God. And God does not call us to misery, sadness, or pain, but to goodness, and joy in his service.

The second special quality is a little more subtle, but it is there just the same. We see holiness in this person not so much as something he himself has attained to, but as something God has given him. We simply see God in him, and somehow realize that this presence of God is a gift. Perhaps the interior sign of this is a certain unconsciousness on the part of the person himself of this special presence of God. We do see this, though, a certain readiness to share this gift of God with others, without, however, the pushiness of the professional evangelist. We also see — and this is the mark of all saints — a quiet confidence in God, a calmness that nothing seems to disturb.

Summing it all up, we may say that our call to be teachers is truly a call from God. In one sense, it is ordinary, in so far as all Christians are called to sanctity, both to live close to God, and to bring others to him. In another sense, however, it is far from ordinary, in so far that ours is a special call to bring Christ to others. And since you can't give away something you don't have, God's call to holiness for others is a call to greater holiness. The call, however, is likewise the gift, so that the holiness that we must attain to is not so much something we give, but something we have been given.

CHAPTER IV
HOLINESS AS RESPONSE

"For these I pray —
not for the world
but for these you have given me,
for they are really yours. . .
I gave them your word,
and the world has hated them for it;
they do not belong to the world
(any more than I belong to the world).
I do not ask you to take them out of the world,
but to guard them from the evil one.
They are not of the world,
any more than I belong to the world.
Consecrate them by means of truth — 'Your
word is truth.'
As you have sent me into the world,
so I have sent them into the world;
I consecrate myself for their sakes now,
that they may be consecrated in truth.
I don't pray for them alone.
I pray also for those who will believe in me
through their word,
that they all may be one
as you, Father, are in me, and I in you;
I pray that they may be (one) in us,
that the world may believe that you sent me"
(Jn 17:9; 14-21).

One of the most memorable scenes in the whole of the Gospel story is that of the Last Supper, as related by St. John, beginning with the fourteenth chapter. We can imagine the solemnity of the occasion, and the silent attention of the apostles as they listened to Jesus speaking to them. He was giving them his last will and testament, and his last admonition, the final declaration of his love. Most impressive of all, however, is the beautiful prayer of chapter seventeen. Jesus prays not that the disciples be shielded from the "world," but from the "evil one" (v. 15); that they be "consecrated in truth" (v. 19); that they and all who believe in him through them may be "one, as you, Father, are in me, and I in you" (v. 21). The prayer of Jesus at the Last Supper, readily sums up the whole idea of holiness: freedom from evil; dedication to "truth," and to all that truth demands of us; unity with God in Christ.

Holiness comes from God. He himself places in us a yearning for spiritual goodness, he instigates the desire to strive for it, he provides the means to attain it. Yet, all of this demands our cooperation. In this chapter, we will look at some of these means of holiness, both as given by God, and as demanding our response.

In the mystery of divine providence, God created man with an intellect to know, and a will to love. In the mystery of this same divine providence, from the beginning, he wished man to use his intellect to know him, and his will to love him. The history of man, however, has shown us that he cannot, by the use of his unaided reason alone, attain to any comprehensive knowledge of God, or any degree of real love. And so, from the beginning, God himself has given man the assistance he has needed. He walked familiarly with Adam and Eve in the garden; he spoke person to person to the patriarchs; he showed his presence to his chosen people for forty years in the desert by signs and revelations; and throughout the next thirteen hundred years, he revealed himself to them through the prophets. Finally, he sent his Son, who became one of us, who spoke to us, who redeemed us, and now in his Church, remains with us. There is a written record of all of this, as we know. It is the Bible, the Sacred Scriptures. This Bible, however, is more than just a record of God's communication with man, more even, than just the means of God "keeping contact." It contains, at least in germ, every facet of the revelation itself, every mode of communication of God to us. It speaks to us of his commandments, his will; it tells us of his presence, his mercy, his love. It is, moreover, no mere history of the past; it is God speaking to us in the here and now. The word of God is a living word, and it comes alive for us today.

Let's go back just to the three points we mentioned as a part of Jesus' prayer, freedom from evil, dedication to truth, unity with God in Christ. The Scriptures are full of instances and expressions, of these needs. The twenty-fifth psalm begins with a prayer for freedom, based on confidence in God. "To you I lift up my soul, O Lord, my God; in you I trust; let me not be put to shame" (v. 1). Upon all of his chosen ones, especially the prophets, God placed the burden of dedication to the truth. Jeremiah, in the twentieth chapter, expresses it most forcefully. "I say to myself, I will not mention him, I will speak in his name no more. But then it becomes like fire burning in my heart, imprisoned in my bones"(v. 9). It is Jesus himself who promises us that we will be one with God. In the fourteenth chapter of St. John's gospel, we hear him say, "Anyone who lives in me will be true to my word, and my Father will love him; we will come to him and make our dwelling place with him" (v. 23). Really, there is no prayer that we can say, no desire, no need that we may have, that is not reflected in the Bible. What makes it such a force in our attainment of holiness?

The Bible is inspired by the Holy Spirit. This means that the Holy Spirit, first of all, picked out certain persons to whom he spoke directly. This need not mean that he "spoke" in the actual sense of the word, but that in some way, perhaps just within the person, he communicated some divine truth, some revelation. Along with this, there was some interior impulse to write — not just to teach. The truth itself, by the way, need not be something new to the writer, but simply revealed to him here and now as something to be written. The Holy Spirit did not "dictate" the book; the writer was left free to use his own style and mode of expression. But the influence of the Holy Spirit was positive, so that the writer expressed the truth in perfect clarity. The Bible is, therefore, the direct communication of God's truth, given by the inspiration of the Holy Spirit.

The Holy Scriptures were inspired to be written. Equally, therefore, they are inspired to be read. We must, however, read them with devotion, with a sincere desire to know the truth. Reading them in this manner, we can be sure that the Holy Spirit will communicate to us the truth that is necessary, helpful, or simply beneficial. We are in as close communication with the Holy Spirit through devout reading of the scriptures as we are with Jesus when we receive Holy Communion.

The Bible is a big book! Just to say, therefore, read the Bible, is for most of us a directive that we are going to find rather hard to follow. In addition, we may be somewhat afraid of beginning to read certain parts of the Bible, especially the Old Testament. For some reason, they have the reputation of being "difficult." It would be a challenge, but a very rewarding one in the end, if we were to sit down and read the Bible cover to cover. An easier way is to select certain parts, the psalms, for example, or the gospels and some of the letters of St. Paul, read — and reread — them, until we become familiar with them and their message. Above all else, read not just to learn, though we may do this, not just to be edified, but that we may be inspired to pray. It is then that the Holy Spirit comes to us, to assist us, to comfort us, to strengthen us, to bring us close to himself, to enable us to rejoice in his presence.

The first definition of prayer that we have learned, and which any kid in the first grade can repeat is "talking to God." Actually, there are as many definitions as there are people to make them. The one that seems to make the most sense, to describe truly just what it is, is to say that prayer is communication. Communication with God. Prayer is, therefore, more than just conversation; more than just dialogue. Communication involves an awareness of the other person, and understanding of him, a comprehension of his deepest feelings. So in true communication, these are mutual, two people are in "conscious contact" with each other, with each other as persons, not just with what each is saying. Such communication can be without words, almost, in fact, without any outward sign at all.

I remember several years ago one of my classmates in ordination had open heart surgery. We had met in high school; and through high school, college, the seminary, and twenty-five years as priests, we remained close friends. The surgery was necessary if he was to live, but when they brought him back, the doctors knew that they had done nothing for him. I think he knew he was going to die. I did. I went to see him, and he held out his right hand, and I took it in both of mine. Neither one of us said a word, but forty years of friendship passed between us in that simple clasp of our hands.

To have this kind of close communication with God requires several things. The first thing it requires is time. We have to take the time to pray, take the time to pray well. Some people speak of praying "all day." That's great — if they really do it. And if they do, I wish they would tell the rest of us how! Living a life as busy, and sometimes as hectic as ours, we wonder, sometimes, if we even have time to think. Most of us are fortunate if we can catch snatches of prayer on the run. For that reason, again, if we are to pray properly, with real devotion, with a sense of real communication with God, we just have to take the time to do it. We need a minimum of ten minutes, off somewhere by ourselves, preferably at the same time every day, someplace where it's quiet. We may begin by just letting ourselves become aware that God is here, that we stand in his presence. We may go forward to the thought, that God loves us — we live in his presence, we live in his love.

Prayer, once again, is communication. Communication in the most perfect manifestation of it, is the mutual revelation of two persons on the deepest level of themselves, of their most intimate being. This kind of communication brings a unity, not just of thought or feeling, but a unity of person. To establish, therefore, this kind of communication in prayer with God is a gift, a gift from him. We make ourselves present to him, we set aside all other thoughts and considerations, we seek this intimate union with him, but he is the one who comes to us. There are times, when we place all the proper attitudes for his coming — and seem to wait in vain for a sense of his presence. But there are also times, when we do feel that presence, suddenly, quietly, but forcefully. When he comes in this manner, we are not so much praying, as in a state of prayer. We are not so much speaking, or even listening, as resting quietly in his presence. Such experiences, though possibly rare, are real. We come back to earth, as it were, but with the memory of his presence and a true sense of contentment. Now we know, for a little while at least, that he is with us, to assist us, to console us, to free us from all evil, to bring us the peace we all are striving for.

It is easy to respond to God's presence when we recognize it deep within us. At such times we would be willing to do anything he might ask us. If our only response to this gift of prayer, however, were the pleasure of the presence of God, the whole thing would be of little value. Real response is in action, action that carries us beyond the experience itself to do the things that God wants us to. St. Francis de Sales says that to make a meditation — such as we have been talking about — and not make a resolution, is like eating all honey and no bread. For this reason, therefore, we can say that God comes to us in this close relationship for more than just to give us a "fuzzy feeling" of pleasure in his company. He comes to inspire us, to strengthen us in the assurance that he is truly with us, to encourage us to make some return to him. The major theme of this book is the call God has given us to bring him to others. Our response, quite naturally, is to accept that call, and to live it, willingly, devoutly, joyfully.

What about the times that we "are there" and God does not make his presence felt? Not only does this happen, but this is what happens frequently. It does not mean that God is disregarding us, rejecting us, or ignoring us. It does mean that the awareness of his coming is a gift, and that he gives it as he wills. We need not be disappointed or discouraged if we do not feel his presence. What is important, however, is that we be ready, we be willing, we respond to his call and his will in whatever way he makes it known.

So far, we have been talking about prayer that is

strictly personal. But prayer not only may be shared, but ought to be shared. We are a "saved people," not just saved persons, and so we go to God as a people. This may be done, however, not only by the whole community of God's people, but also by certain special groups, such as the community formed by the religion teachers of the parish to which we belong. We are not excluding others involved in the religious education program, including the students, but for our present purpose, we wish to speak only of us as teachers. Because of our dedication to a special task, we do form a special community, and as such may and ought to go to God to seek his assistance for our common needs together.

We can recall the oft-quoted words of our Lord who said, "Where two or three are gathered in my name, there am I in their midst" (Mt 18:20). As teachers engaged in a common endeavor to bring Christ to others, we really ought to take these words seriously. We have said much about the call that God has given us individually, the gifts he has given us to live up to it, and our need to respond to it with generosity. But all of us, sharing as we do a common task of bringing Christ to the students in our own parish school of religion, have been called by God together to fulfill a common purpose. Since prayer is our response to God, then it may and should be a shared response.

How do we go about it? One of the things that we may find helpful is to organize an informal prayer group among the teachers who teach the same day and time session. This need not be anything "big." At our parish, we have a short informal gathering after each class, and we begin with a few minutes of sharing of some of the things that went on in class, amusing, embarrassing, serious, inspirational. One of us reads a short passage from the Bible, and explains briefly what it means to him. Each of us may also respond. We close with a moment of silence and a blessing.

It sounds simple enough doesn't it, as though nothing much would come of it? Yet, over the course of just a few months, and certainly over the year, there has come to our teachers a unity, a closeness, a mutual understanding that never existed before. An added value, especially for our newer teachers, is a greater awareness of the Bible as a source of prayer and inspiration, and a freedom in sharing their own thoughts and feelings in prayer.

Prayer is just one of the gifts God gives us to respond to him. He has also given us the seven signs we call sacraments. These, too, are among the gifts wherein we must do something in order to receive them. God does not just pour the graces of the sacraments into us as if he were filling up a bottle. We have to receive them. To receive them most fully, we need to be adequately prepared and spiritually awake.

It is not our purpose in this discussion to explain the sacraments, or their theological significance. Instead, we want to try to show how they affect our spiritual life, how they bring us closer to God. This is important, especially for us who are called to teach others.

The definition of a sacrament that we all learned in our catechism, "an outward sign, instituted by Christ, to give grace," is adequate. It does not, however, tell us anything of the personal nature of a sacrament. Sacraments are an "encounter with Christ." The basic effect, therefore, is that Christ comes to us in person in each of them; he comes to make us one with him, he comes to fulfill our need of the moment. From the beginning of history, man has always sought some way to be close to his God. God himself, having made man, understood that, and has fulfilled this need in the whole of salvation history. At the very beginning, he walked familiarly with the man and woman he created. He spoke directly to the patriarchs; he stayed with and protected his people throughout their history, even when they abandoned him in sin. He sent his Son to live with us, to be one of us. He continues to fulfill that basic need of ours, coming to us in person in the sacraments. It is because of this divine coming that we receive the "grace," the holiness of the sacrament.

This is the gift, the holiness offered us by God. But to this, we must respond, we must take it up. Since it is Christ who comes to us in person, we must welcome him personally. We ought, therefore, to come alive in his presence. As in so many other spiritual things, this means awareness. Awareness begins with recollection, recollection of what the sacrament means, recollection of who it is we receive. We will try to see, therefore, what his living presence means to us, as persons and as teachers, in the four sacraments that are most familiar to us: Baptism, Confirmation, Eucharist and Reconciliation.

St. Paul, in the letter to the Romans, has this to say, "Are you not aware that we who were baptized into Christ Jesus were baptized into his death? Through baptism into his death we were buried with him, so that just as Christ was raised from the dead by the glory of the Father, we too might live a new life" (6:3-4). We have all heard the explanation of baptism as a washing — as the body is "washed" with water, so the soul is cleansed from sin. As lucid as this explanation is, the one we have just quoted from St. Paul is by far the most meaningful and accurate. In baptism, we die and are buried to the life of sin in imitation of the death and burial of Christ, and with him we rise from the dead. This symbol is most perfectly carried out, of course, in baptism through immersion. But even if this ceremony is no longer the usual manner of baptizing, death, burial and resurrection best portray the real meaning of the sacrament.

Through this symbolism, we see the first effect of the sacrament, freedom from sin, from the force of sin. This freedom is effected in us whether we are infants, and need only liberation from original sin, or whether we are adults, and need freedom from our own sins as well. For adults who are baptized, this freedom involves a renunciation of sin, a renunciation that is not just for the moment, but is permanent, lasting, and complete. For this reason, we Christians live in the permanent state of this freedom from sin. As in all spiritual things, the power to be free comes from God, but requires our cooperation.

Death, without a resurrection, in my interpretation, is meaningless. So also, in baptism, the concomitant effect, resurrection, is equally important. We rise to the new life of grace, to the new life of God himself, we become sharers in the divine life itself, we have the power to live and act on the divine level. What this means for us is written by St. Peter in his first letter. "You are a chosen race, a royal priesthood, a holy nation, a people he claims for his own to proclaim the glorious works of the One who has called you from darkness into his marvelous light" (2:19). We are, indeed, through baptism, a people set apart, made holy by our union with Christ through his resurrection. Salvation comes to us through the Church, the People of God. For that reason, we ought to remember that all of the divine gifts that do come to us do so because of our belonging to that saved people. The call, therefore, that comes to us is a call to be joined to "this holy nation, this royal priesthood, this people set apart." To be a Christian, therefore, is to realize that we truly belong to one another in Christ.

We can see from this, one of the things, we, as

teachers, hope to impart to our students. We seek to bring them to the consciousness that they are not alone, that Christ comes to them through their unity with the community. It will help to form this idea in their minds if we can begin to form the class into a "mini-community," a consciousness that they are one, with us as well as with each other. This is not something that we can legislate, manipulate, or decree. This is something that must simply "happen." But we can begin to make it happen if we truly seek the good of each person in our class, see each one of them as persons, relate to each of their needs.

The ceremonies that accompany the rite of Baptism bring out this idea of community. In addition, they highlight some important effects of the sacrament besides the gift of life. In the new rite, the water is blessed at each baptism, in order to remind us of the many ways that God has used water in the history of salvation. Especially recalled are the renewal of the human race through Noah after the deluge, the salvation of the chosen people through the passage of the Red Sea, the baptism of Jesus himself, and the water that flowed from his side when he was pierced by a lance. All of these are intended to point out to us the truths that salvation ultimately comes from God, and that his saving power will be among us perpetually, without interruption until the end of time.

There is a part of the ceremony that has a great amount of meaning, but which sometimes evokes little response from even the parents and godparents, let alone any of the congregation who are present. This is the renewal of the baptismal promises. If we examine them, we find that they are a capsule description of the Christian, and therefore whenever the opportunity to renew them is presented to us, we may make them for ourselves. Just briefly, let us see what they mean.

"Reject sin, and live in the freedom of God's children." There is an important point here, that to keep the commandments and so to be able to keep from committing sin is not a burden, but a freedom, a freedom that belongs to the children of God, a gift, really, that he gives us as his children.

"Reject the glamour of evil." This is one of the real signs of maturity, to be able to see through the apparent good of all the things most people today consider most important: wealth, position, pleasure. These things, as well as sin itself, have glamour. We all need that gift of maturity to place them in their proper perspective.

"Reject Satan, the father of sin and prince of darkness." The devil is real, and there is no doubt about that. St. Peter calls him a "roaring lion, seeking someone to devour" (1 P 5:8). We have all experienced his power when we have been subject to temptations that could have come from nowhere except the pit of hell.

Two things come to mind. The next time we are witnesses of a baptism, which takes place at a Sunday Mass, at the time of the promises, speak out! It always disturbs me whenever I have a baptism at Mass, to hear no more than a weak "I do" over here, and another over there, and this from a whole congregation of people! Whenever the call comes to profess ourselves as Christians, stand up and be counted! Secondly, we can teach the children, especially those preparing for any of the sacraments, the real meaning behind these simple promises. We can also use them, not only as a part of the lesson, but a part of the class prayer, more to demonstrate the holiness that they mean and can lead us to.

There are three ceremonies after the actual baptism which have a great amount of meaning both as demonstrating the gifts of the sacrament, and as reminders of what it is to be a follower of Christ. The prayer of the anointing with chrism recalls the three-fold role of Christ, of priest, prophet, and king — in which we have a share. We may recall that we share in the priestly role by accepting the sacrifices of daily living in union with the sacrifice of Christ, as well as by our participation in the Mass. We share in the prophetic role, especially as teachers, by our proclamation of Christ's kingdom, both by teaching and by living a Christian life. We share in the royal role by our untiring efforts to bring about a more just distribution of this world's goods to all others. This is not just a passing duty, this is a way of life.

The priest puts a white garment, the symbol of Christ, on the newly baptized, and says, "you have become a new creation, and have clothed yourself in Christ." Christ in us is to be as visible to others as the clothes we wear. Then we light the baptismal candle, the symbol of ourselves, from the Easter candle, the symbol of Christ living in his Church. This light, in the words of Jesus, must "shine before men" (Mt 5:16). These two symbols, the white garment and the light, proclaim to the world that we belong to Christ, we live in Christ, we seek to make him known and loved.

"I will pour out my spirit upon all mankind. Your sons and daughters shall prophesy, your old men shall dream dreams, your young men shall see visions; even upon the servants and the handmaids, in those days, I will pour out my spirit" (Jl 3:1-3). These are the words of the prophet Joel, quoted by St. Peter on the day of Pentecost, when, in his address to the people of Jerusalem, he was explaining what took place with the apostles. The Holy Spirit had come upon them and transformed them into entirely different men. From "ignorant fishermen" afraid of their very lives, they suddenly became, by the power of the Spirit poured out upon them, men enlightened in faith and strong in courage. It is in the dramatic transformation that we may see what the Sacrament of Confirmation brings into our lives.

Confirmation is the sacrament of the Holy Spirit, first of all. This does not mean that the Holy Spirit is not given with the first gift of grace, as, for instance, at baptism, but it does mean that in Confirmation his grace is poured out on us in a manner that is special, his power is given in a more forceful way, his presence is realized in us by a more vivid awareness. This outpouring of the Holy Spirit is the primary effect of Confirmation, and, fittingly, is primarily demonstrated by the sign of the sacrament. The Apostolic Constitution on the new rite states that the sacrament is given through the anointing with oil, which is done by the laying on of hands. From Old Testament times, the anointing with oil and the laying on of hands has always signified a special consecration to God, the conferring of a special gift. Here the sign of the Sacrament both signifies the outpouring of the Holy Spirit, and actually brings about his presence. From this moment on, we begin to be different. No longer are we just Christians, but we are Christians endowed with the special power and presence of the Holy Spirit. This power, this presence, moreover, is permanent. The bishop says to us, "Be sealed with the gift of the Holy Spirit." Be sealed — with a seal that is permanent as our souls, that now and forever sets us apart as one in whom the Holy Spirit has taken up permanent residence.

Confirmation is the sacrament of the apostle. During his life on earth, both before and after the resurrection, Jesus conferred on his apostles special spiritual powers, among them full spiritual authority over the whole world. By the very command of Jesus himself, however, these powers were held in abeyance until they should have received "power from on high" (Lk 24:49). Filled with the Holy Spirit, they threw open the doors of the room where they were locked in, and boldly proclaimed the name of Jesus. As confirmed Christians, filled, as were the power and grace of the Holy Spirit, we also are sent to proclaim the name of the Lord. As those called to the special task of teaching, we may expect two things. The call, indeed, the interior demand to proclaim Christ to others will be more positive, while the outpouring of the grace, the very presence of the Holy Spirit, will be more clearly felt.

Confirmation is called the sacrament of maturity. We grow up in Christ. For all the attractiveness of babies, no one really wants to stay a baby all his life. In fact, one of the most frequent expressions we hear, especially when we are acting less than adults, is, "Why don't you grow up?" This maturity is marked by two things, both of which are also gifts of the Holy Spirit. We grow up to a certain measure of wisdom. Understanding this wisdom as a Gift, we have the facility of seeing all things that happen in our lives as God sees them. It is the facility to see through appearances to the reality of what our lives ought to be. The second is the gift of fortitude. Through this gift, we stand before the world as confirmed Christians, firm in faith, firm in the dedication to do always what is right. When the call comes for Christians — real Christians, firm in the conviction of faith and the meaning of goodness — we are able to stand among them.

These are not negligible powers or graces. We all realize this, so much so, in fact, that there are few Catholic adults who are not confirmed, and even fewer who do not insist that their children receive the sacrament. For most of us, however, it seems to stop there. We don't come alive to the presence of the Holy Spirit. Without a doubt, this is our greatest need.

Having been confirmed, we respond to the presence of the Spirit with the sure conviction that he is constantly at work in us.

At work in us he is, indeed. We feel that power sometimes at prayer, when very simply, our minds and hearts seem to respond to him with greater conviction. We feel it in response to prayer, when, perhaps we are searching for enlightenment. We feel it in study, when some old truth suddenly has a new meaning or a new clarity. We feel it as we prepare to teach, when an idea for presenting this same truth to our students just comes to us. We know it is there, even as we teach, when right in the middle of a lesson, one of these insights comes to us in such perfect context with the lesson, that we scarcely drop a vowel. The Holy Spirit is in us, and he works in us. We can depend on it.

At work, he is in the students, too. We ought not to sell this short. If the Holy Spirit is going to make himself felt in us to teach more effectively, more clearly, and with greater wisdom, surely he is going to be in the students to enable them to grasp the truth with greater clarity and firmness. Without stretching the truth at all, there is a perfect parallel here with the action of the Holy Spirit in his inspiration of the Sacred Scriptures, and, in fact, with the Church as a whole. His inspiration effects both those who proclaim the message and those who receive.

The obvious response to all of this is to pray for the power and grace of the Holy Spirit, that he may truly work in us and in our students. But first, we have to be convinced that his power and grace is in us. This is where we have to start. Be convinced that his presence is in us first of all for ourselves, so that we may personally come closer to him in truth, in goodness, in love. Having been awakened in the Spirit, but only having first been awakened in the Spirit, we may be sure that we have the power to communicate him to others.

Surely, if there is one way to sanctify, both as individuals and as members of the Christian community, it is the gift of God's intimate union with us in the Holy Eucharist. The Holy Eucharist is a sacrifice and a sacrament. Under the appearances of bread and wine, the Lord Jesus in person is offered and received. This definition sounds simple, but it is full of meaning. Most importantly, the Holy Eucharist is the presence of Jesus in person, the living, risen Jesus. It is not necessary here to discuss the theological aspects of the manner of Jesus' presence, for example, by transubstantiation. It is not necessary to establish "proof" of his presence, as is customarily done by reciting the words of promise of institution. Rather, let us try to see something of the meaning of the reality of Jesus' presence in the Holy Eucharist. We will discuss three aspects: the divine Presence itself, the renewal of his sacrifice, and Communion.

We may begin by recalling the growth in faith in Jesus by his chosen "twelve." Roughly, it went from simply recognizing Jesus as one chosen by God, to a prophet, to Messiah, to Son of God. But more than this, recall the intimacy they enjoyed with him, His special admonitions, his special revelations, his special concern. Along with this, they held the hope that he would be the one to restore Israel. We can imagine, therefore, the joy and satisfaction of sharing in the triumphal procession of Palm Sunday. All the more shattering, therefore, was the experience of Good Friday. The whole thing was wiped out! Talk about a traumatic experience! And after a day of bewildered sadness came Easter Sunday! St. John describes it best (Ch. 20). As soon as Mary Magdalene who had been to the tomb reported to the apostles that it was empty, Peter and John ran there — *ran* there. We can imagine what was in their minds, especially as they began to recall that Jesus promised that he would rise from the dead. When they got there, they saw the cloths that had covered his body neatly folded and "they believed" (v. 8).

Now let's go forward a week or two after the coming of the Holy Spirit. He had endowed the apostles with "power from on high" (Lk 24:49). Joyfully and enthusiastically they went out shouting the good news that the Jesus whom they had put to death had now risen, that he was truly Son of God and Messiah.

On the evening of the Sabbath — recall that they still considered themselves a part of the Jewish community — the disciples of Jesus would come together for the traditional end of the Sabbath meal. Imagine the joy of reunion; the enthusiasm as they told each other about their preaching, the conversions, the miracles, the miracles of grace — the whole bundle of the funny, the sad, the insulting and the inspiring. As the meal progressed, the time would come for the cup of thanksgiving, and one of them would take bread, and in memory of Jesus say the words of Jesus, "Take this and eat it, this is my Body" (Mt 26:26). And Jesus would be there! Not just in memory, but in person. And they would feel his presence, not just each within himself, but in the community of all of them gathered together. We may sense the hush that would surround his presence, the memories that would flood their minds, the renewal of the strength to continue, the confidence to face all things. Here, they began to understand his promise that he would be with them always, "until the end of the world" (Mt 28:20). Jesus was present, and his presence would remain.

This is what has come down to us. As the members of the original group who began to spread the gospel message to distant places, they never failed to gather their new members together to celebrate the "Lord's Supper." Into each of these gatherings, throughout nineteen centuries, Jesus came — as into each of our gatherings he comes today. We, as the apostles did, may have the same sense of Jesus' presence with us in the community, and in fact, it is essential that we do so. This is the first meaning of the Mass, the union of the community of Jesus.

The Church has always insisted that this is the real meaning of the Mass — the offerings of the community of God's people with the priest of the renewal of the sacrifice of Christ on the cross. Before the changes in the liturgy, however, that was not the way we "assisted" at it. We were silent spectators. Even at "High Mass," when parts were sung, the priest had to recite these same parts privately. Now, however, with the "new liturgy," we may feel that we are truly sharing in the actual offering of the sacrifice. More importantly, we experience the sense of oneness with the priest and with each other.

As a priest, I, personally, see the difference. In the "old Mass," I strived for a sense of unity with Christ. Now as I offer the sacrifice, I strive for and feel a sense of unity with the congregation as together we go to God. This is not always easy, frankly, on Sundays with a large and diverse congregation. However, it never fails to take place at the celebration of a Mass for some special occasion, for some special group, such as the Mass of thanksgiving for our teachers at the end of the school year. This Mass is ours, and it has the God-given power to make us truly one.

In the eucharistic liturgy, we share in offering the sacrifice of Christ, with Christ, and with one another. Here we share in the priestly role of Christ. Christ was victim as well as priest, and so fully to share in his priestly role means to share in his role of victim as well.

This we may do right at the Mass, when we may say with the priest during the preparation prayers, "Lord God, we ask you to receive us" (Sacramentary). This is a beautiful prayer, and a rather easy one to say. It becomes a little tougher when the prayer becomes a reality, instead of a simple offering of our wills, we must make it in person. The opportunities for being a true victim with Christ are manifold; we just have to keep our eyes open to them. This is not to say that our lives are necessarily a "vale of tears," but it is to say that the opportunity for the sacrifice of accepting God's will is frequent — and not always easy.

We carry the logic of our share in the priestly role of Christ one step further. The sacrifice he offered was a redeeming act — it was for us and our salvation. So also may ours be a redeeming act. St. Paul says, "even now I find my joy in the suffering I endure for you. In my own flesh I fill up what is lacking in the sufferings of Christ for the sake of his body, the church" (Col 1:24). There is a great amount of theological truth in this, as well as a great understanding of the value of suffering for others. Very simply, we may say that Christ won for us the grace of redemption by the sufferings of his physical body, he continues to confer that grace through the sufferings of his Mystical Body, that is, through us, who are his members.

From the beginning, man has always sought some way to be close to God, to be sure of his benevolence. Sacrifice, for example, even the sacrifice of appeasement, has been offered for this purpose. God himself knows this, and in the history of salvation, has continuously shown his presence, to fulfill this wish, to give reassurance, to show mankind his love and mercy. The person of Christ represents the ultimate intimacy, the fulness of the gift of God and the satisfaction of man's desire. The promise of Jesus comes true in the actual meaning of the words, that he will live with us and we with him (Jn 6:56). But more than this, by the very fact that each one of us is united to our Lord, we are thereby made one with each other, in as close and intimate union as is possible. We have heard this a thousand times, and we know that it is true. At the same time, somehow or other, it just never occurs to us, even at the time of Communion. What are we going to do about it? One thing that we can do is to awaken our minds and hearts at the sign of peace. Not just to smile and shake hands, though this is a big improvement over things as they were, but to have a sense of closeness to the person, especially to one who belongs to us. Then, in our moment's reflection after Communion, we can recall that now we are actually one with Jesus and with each other. We believe it, we make it alive.

There are many applications of this. Those who are married, and are parents of children, can make family Communion a real source of unity, a real source of wanting goodness for each other, a real source of cooperation, a real source of love. These are not just a lot of pretty expressions; these things can happen, if we just become aware of the meaning of our being made one in Christ. This we can teach our students, and if we have a "class Mass," we can help them to have this sense of being one with Christ and each other. As teachers, we can have that same oneness with each other whenever we participate at Mass together.

These three aspects, the divine Presence, the Sacrifice, and Communion, coalesce into one. It is the one Jesus who has come to us and is present to us. We divide these aspects, at least in our minds, but there is no division in the fact of Jesus' presence. That's why Mass — and this means Mass and Communion — is so important. That is why it is even more important that whenever we come to Mass we not only know what the

Mass is, but that we are aware right here and now of what we are about. Vatican II, in the *Constitution on the Liturgy*, (nn. 10 and 11) brings out some beautiful and telling points. It says, "From the liturgy, and especially from the Eucharist, grace is poured forth upon us as a fountain." It also says, though, that for this fountain of grace to fully refresh us, we must approach it with the proper dispositions, well aware of what we are doing. This seems like nothing new, because "proper dispositions" has always been the one necessary condition for reception of communion, provided we are in the "state of grace." But the fathers of Vatican II mean a little more here. They mean that deep understanding, that deep awareness of all that we know that the Eucharist can mean to us. They mean that we ought to be awake at the moment we receive, that it is Jesus who is present, who makes us live in him, who makes us truly one with each other. For this we need reflection: reflection on the meaning of Jesus' presence right at the time he comes. We need reflection at other times as well, and need times of silent prayer during the day. These are the times, especially, when we may be refreshed at the fountain of the Eucharist, refreshed by the memory of Jesus, by the presence of Jesus, who lives in us with his love.

If there is one thing that strikes us about the sacrament of Penance — or Reconciliation, as it is now called — it is the wide variety of opinion it has collected; some of it contradictory, about its value. In no way can we even try to reconcile all or any of these opinions, but we can try to see some of the truths about the sacrament that will help us see it in relation to the fact of sanctity, to God's intention to bring us closer to him. The purpose of the sacrament, and therefore, the center around which everything about it revolves, is freedom from sin. We generally think of sin as sinful actions, whereby we offend God and hurt others. This understanding of sin is accurate, but we may also consider sin as *sinfulness*, a weakening of our nature, certain "character defects" or traits of personality. Because of this *sinfulness*, actions become easy for us. The power of the redeeming death of Jesus brought our freedom from this *sinfulness*, and so also does the sacrament of reconciliation.

One of the most consoling truths of our faith is the mercy of God, the love of God shown in forgiveness. The whole history of salvation, in fact, from the sin of our first parents, is a history of just that, of forgiveness. For this reason, the Sacrament of Reconciliation is one of his most precious gifts. Since it is our purpose to speak about the sacraments in their relationship to God's special call to holiness, we will try to confine our discussion to this relationship, reconciliation and the special call of God. We will begin with the fact of sin, the one thing that keeps us from God. The reason for this is that sin is a fact, sin is real in our lives.

In order to see sin in its proper light, let us take a look at man in the state of sinlessness, the state of original perfection. God made man in the state of perfect goodness, not only free from sin, but free from sinfulness, free from any internal leaning or drive toward sin. We see man in the state, therefore, of perfect harmony, harmony with himself, with each other, and with God. We say that man was in the state of full integrity, in full possession of all of his powers. The Bible indicates this when it says that "the man and his wife were both naked, yet they felt no shame" (Gn 2:25). Being in perfect harmony within themselves, the man and his wife were in perfect harmony with each other. There is no direct indication of this in the Bible account, but we may make a safe conjecture that this was so both from the fact that they went naked, and from the fact that Adam recognized Eve as being a part of himself, and therefore his perfect equal. Most certainly, however, was man in harmony with God. God spoke with him person to person, and was accustomed to walk with him in "the breezy time of day" (Gn 3:8).

Sin destroyed the whole thing. As soon as they ate of the forbidden fruit, "the eyes of both of them were opened, and they realized that they were naked" (Gn 3:7). Immediately upon sinning, they felt a deep sense of shame, and along with a sense of guilt. Man had turned against himself. But this was not all. There occurred a division between them as well. When God questioned the man about his sin, immediately he blamed his wife. Peace between man and man was broken, and as long as sin stays in the world, it will never be repaired. Fear now takes the place of the beautiful harmony between God and man. "I heard you in the garden; but I was afraid, because I was naked, so I hid myself" (Gn 3:10). In spite of all the testimonies of God's love, in history and in our personal lives, we have never really gotten free of that first fear of God. Sin, therefore, is the one destructive, divisive force in our lives.

We may apply all of these effects of sin to ourselves. How many times when we have done something wrong, something really wrong, such as a secret act of vengeance, have we said to ourselves, "I hate myself!" Or how many times have we fallen back into the same sin, and wondered how we could have been so "stupid?" How many times have we carried the guilt of a sin so terrible — at least in our minds — that we have buried it in shame in the depths of our soul? Indeed, sin splits us down the middle, turns us, as it were, into spiritual schizophrenics.

Sin divides us from each other. One simple example: If I tell you a lie, I set up a wall between us. I am afraid of you. I never feel comfortable with you. I am constantly worried that you will find out the truth. And if you do find out the truth, then you lose trust in me. Sin indeed is a destructive, divisive force between us.

Sin splits us off from God. Sin engenders a sense of shame, a sense of guilt, a sense of fear. The fact that we have been brought up with the idea of sin and punishment, that every sin must in some way be accounted for, does not help any. There are some persons who have doubted the fact of divine forgiveness, and some who have worried about their past sins to their dying day. Sin divides us from God, with a division that can be lasting, that can really hurt.

The redeeming power of the life, death, and resurrection of Jesus is the ultimate, the divinely given means freeing us from the fact of sin. Full freedom, demands more than just "forgiveness," even divine forgiveness. It demands a full repair of the triple breach caused by the sin, a repair we may call reconciliation. We might point out here that sin comes from within us, from our interior desires. Jesus brought this out in one of his discourses, saying that "not what goes into a man makes him unclean, but what comes out, because what comes out comes from the heart" (Mk 8:21-23). Reconciliation likewise, therefore, must take place *within* us. We begin by seeing ourselves as we really are. We are quite used to what we have called an "examination of conscience." In this act we take a look at what we have done, at the individual sinful acts. What we really need, however, is a much greater, a much deeper penetration into ourselves. What we do, therefore, is take our attention away from what we have done, and place it on ourselves, the person. I say to myself, not "I have done these things," but, "I am the person who has done these things." In other words, I accept the responsibility not just for my actions, but for me, the person. In so doing, I recognize one important truth, that I am responsible for myself, that I freely made myself who I am. To come to this acceptance of ourselves, requires a great amount of self honesty. When I begin to see myself as I am, however, and accept the truth of who I am, there comes to me a sense of redemption, a sense of freedom. If I freely made myself into who I am, I am equally free at this moment to make myself into a different person. Not just that I am free not to do sinful things again, but that *I am free to be truly different*. It is this different person who does not do these sinful acts.

Now I can go back to God. I can ask his forgiveness, I can be reconciled, I can again be one with him. Now I can be reconciled to others. I can apologize. The new person that I am trying to become will have a power with others to bring them back to me, to bring them close to me, that words alone can not effect. Now, too, I can be free of my past within myself. I don't have to salve my conscience with phony excuses, that I wasn't thinking, that I didn't mean it. Going back to the beginning, I simply accept the responsibility for being me, but am satisfied and calm with the knowledge that I can become a different "me."

The new rite of the sacrament of reconciliation, or as our second graders are taught to call it, the sacrament of peace, is designed to bring about freedom on three levels. The priest is instructed immediately to greet the penitent with kindness, to recall for him the loving mercy of God, and to encourage him to have confidence. The scripture reading has the same purpose, and the selections suggested center around the fact of God's merciful forgiveness. All of this we have heard before, but right now, it is time for us to bring the truth of God's mercy down from the purely intellectual level to the level of internal feeling, the level of personal conviction. There is no such thing as an unforgiveable sin, just as there is no such thing as an unforgiveable sinner. It is true that we have to go back to God with full and honest recognition of our sinfulness, and with the true desire to be a new person. Once, however, we have sincerely turned back to God, he will receive us with mercy and love. His forgiveness, moreover, is complete. He holds nothing further against us. We need not spend any time in fear that some calamity will happen to us in "punishment." Once he forgives, he forgives.

Formerly, in confession we categorized our sins, telling each by "name, rank, and number." In other words, "just the facts." The new instruction tells us to speak "in a conversational tone," and now we may simply "tell it like it is." We may also confess our character defects, our general attitudes, our habits of failure in our love of God or others. All of this is a part of that honesty which is essential for personal freedom from the sense of sin that has filled us with shame, and guilt, and destroyed our peace of mind.

Satisfaction in the revised rite — the penance we always said — likewise takes on a new understanding, and so may take on a new form. Sin destroys personal unity with others. We need to be reconciled, and this reconciliation can be a part of the rite itself. As penitents, we may suggest to the priest what we think would be adequate satisfaction, especially when we have injured others. Some apology, therefore, some kindness, to let the other person know that we wish to be restored to his good graces.

This sacrament, therefore, rightly understood and received, is a true means of reconciliation, with God, with others, within ourselves. And rightly understood, it is surely one of God's greatest gifts. This is the sacrament of reconciliation, of repair, of healing, of peace. Hopefully, therefore, we can get over our fears, our hang-ups, our disinclination of receiving this sacrament, and approach it calmly, confidently, even joyfully.

Time now for a little recapitulation. The call to be Christians, as Vatican II has told us, is a call to sanctity. The special call to be teachers of religion is, therefore, a call to greater sanctity. In issuing this call, God has bestowed on us two sets of supernatural powers. One of these is the infused gifts of grace, the virtues, the Gifts of the Holy Spirit. The other is the means of holiness offered to us to use, prayer and the sacraments. Since the teaching of religion is the communication of the whole of Christian living, and not just the facts of faith, then what we communicate to our students is not just "catechism," but the value of these God-given means of coming close to him. St. Thomas says, *"Nemo dat quod non habet,"* or as we say in plain English, "You can't give away something you don't have." We, therefore, must use these same means to come close to God ourselves. Then, at least in the striving, if not in the fulfillment, we will be able to communicate the truth, the value, the reality of the holiness that we call Christian living.

CHAPTER V
ONE TOGETHER

Behold, how good it is, and how pleasant,
where brethen dwell at one!
It is when the precious ointment
  upon the head
runs down over the beard, the beard
  of Aaron,
till it runs down upon the collar of his
  robe.
It is a dew like that of Hermon,
which comes down upon the mountains
  of Zion;
for there the Lord has pronounced
  his blessing,
life forever (Psalm 133).

"Behold, how good it is, and how pleasant,
Where brethren dwell at one! . . ." (Ps 133:1)
All of us respond to these words of the psalm, perhaps because it is an ideal to be striven for rather than an accomplished state. Yet, to some degree at least, we know that the ideal is valid, having experienced a beautiful harmony with others. As teachers working to bring Christ to our young people, not in isolation, but in a cohesive program, there is need for a true spirit of community. Community in its basic definition is the working of two or more together to attain a single goal.
Community, however — real community — is much more than that. The simplest and best descrip-

tion comes from the Acts of the Apostles, "The community of believers were of one heart and one mind" (Ac 4:32). One heart and one mind says everything. There is more than just unity of purpose here, or even unity of individuals working for a common goal. Here there is a real unity of persons. In other words, we have to distinguish between the fact of real community from the working together to attain a common goal.

There is a lot these two things have in common, and we might be deceived into thinking we have community, when we have only a common striving for a single purpose. In any common endeavor, we have to start off with a single purpose, a single goal. It is self evident that the final result of anything we want to do has got to be the first thing in our minds, in our intention. In other words, every single member of the group must be bound together by a singleness of purpose, each one knowing and striving for the one goal of the whole group. Secondly, there must be a spirit of cooperation. Not only must each know where the whole group is going, but sincerely work, and work together to get there. A true spirit of cooperation demands that each one set aside his own personal ideas and ambitions for the sake of the singleness of purpose of the whole.

Finally, there ought to be a spirit of helpfulness, of assistance one for another. Since attainment of the goal is the first consideration of all, mutual assistance must be given and received without any suggestion of criticism. Idealistic as all of this is, the true spirit of community goes beyond it.

The basic difference between working together for a single purpose and community is that in community there is a unity of persons. This special unity of persons is not something one "builds," the result of a set purpose, as if one were to say, "Let's have a community." Community happens. Community happens when two or more people begin to share not just their time and talents for a single purpose, but begin to share themselves. How does this come about? It is really hard to say, but we may trace the process along these general lines.

Two persons begin to form a community when they begin to recognize the personal values and goodness in the other, and proceed from here to a respect for the person himself. Each sees the other as a person, not just as one who is contributing to a purpose, and both of them are drawn to each other as persons. This is followed by a desire to know the other better, and at the same time to be better known. Right here we are at the point of decision, although we may not avert to the fact. We begin to open up ourselves to each other, tell each other who we really are, and accept our mutual response. Psychologists tell us that this action is a "risk." We see it as a freely given gift. None of this can be planned, certainly not manipulated. Community depends upon freedom, the freedom of friendship, really the freedom of love. How good and how pleasant is true community, where "brothers dwell as one."

What a beautiful religious education program we would all have if everybody involved formed a true community! In fact, without true community we could question the worth of our efforts. We have an advantage over those engaged in purely mundane endeavors. Our call is to fulfill a purpose that is spiritual, supernatural, divine. We have been called to be ourselves formed in Christ, as well as to form others in Christ, through constant growth in faith and holiness. We are involved in religious education, and education is essentially growth. We ourselves may not ever stop learning, may never stop seeing Christ more clearly in our lives, may never stop seeking to grow closer to him. This will always be our individual goal. When this is the common goal of everyone involved in the program in which we share, each of us is strengthened by the support of all the others.

Here we may apply the principle of "synergism." Very simply, synergism means that the "whole is greater than the sum of its parts." This may not sound very mathematical, but it is true even in material things. The perfect hexagonals that make up a bee hive are ounce by ounce far stronger than the same amount of material built haphazardly. In groups of people, ideas and suggestions that come from the group working together far supersede in content and value the sum total of all the ideas of the individuals working alone. The cooperation at least, if not a real community, of teachers dedicated to a common goal is certainly an immense advantage, almost a necessity. Several points may illustrate this.

First and foremost, community means that we are not alone. Nothing can be more shattering to our confidence than to have no place to turn, no one to go to. On the other hand, there is no security like the security of knowing that there are others who are ready and willing to help us. This is the experience of all of us. And it is perfectly human. The realization of the importance of the task demands the strengthening power of the assurance that others can help, sometimes only that others are there. A spirit of unity and cooperation, therefore, among all the persons involved in a certain program is an advantage that we very much need. Once again, we are strengthened and encouraged by the fact — we are not alone.

The first level of actual cooperation is for the teachers of the same grade to plan their lessons together. It doesn't take much to see the mutual advantage of this. Let's go back to our principle of synergism, that is, that a group working together has a higher power of production than the sum total of all the same individuals working separately. One reason for this comes immediately to our minds, in the field of ideas. We not only share ideas, but we build on each other's, and progress in a kind of ascending spiral. In addition, there is engendered a real spirit of cooperation and helpfulness. This is especially important, and even necessary for new teachers, not only to assist them in their teaching, but to give them the needed confidence that they may receive help whenever they want or need it. Once again, we are never alone.

While, however, this spirit of cooperation is almost a must for teachers of the same grade level, it extends itself to everybody in the program. A smooth running program requires a cooperation on the practical level: first of all, in the matters of orderliness, neatness, proper use of materials and keeping the basic rules. Cooperation is also required among the different grades in the matter of the doctrine taught. The program is designed to be a unified whole. Each level ought to be conscious of fulfilling its own part toward the attainment of the goal of the entire program.

A real *spirit* of cooperation, however, is always on a personal basis. Since this is so, we cannot accurately pinpoint all the ways in which this cooperation is manifested. At the same time, there are a few things which are clearly manifestations of it. The first of these is mutual respect — to be able to see each other with our own particular attitudes, ideas, personalities. To put this in reverse, we accept each other without criticism. Secondly, we are willing to listen. One of the most important needs that any person has is the need to be listened to. Obviously, therefore, somebody has to listen. And how hard it is to find anyone willing to listen! How often are we telling some incident of interest to us, and how impatient the other person is to interrupt and relate some experience of his own? If this takes place in a group, and something causes a distraction, how impossible to pick up the thread of the story! The third thing is to be open to the needs of others, to respond to their need, whenever it may occur, and whatever it may be. This requires a sensitivity to others not found in very many of us naturally. We have to develop it. We begin by having an interest in them as persons, by simply being aware of them. From here we need to develop a sensitivity to their "need of the moment." Perhaps all they need is a kind word; perhaps all they need is for us to go away and leave them alone! Here is where sensitivity is necessary — to see and respond to their need, not our idea about how we ought to help.

When we take a look at all of this, we are describing one mode of Christian love. Christian love is most perfectly manifested seeking goodness for others; goodness, moreover, on every possible level. Because we love them, and not ourselves, we are willing to put ourselves aside for their greater good. Cooperation and communication on levels as deep as these is the beginning of true community.

Of all the things, however, that can bring us together, enable us to cooperate with each other, and to build true community, is shared prayer. This should come as no surprise to any of us, because we are all familiar with the words of Jesus, "Where two or three are gathered in my name, there am I in their midst" (Mt 18:20). The most obvious effects of this sharing in prayer are that as we pray together we become more aware of our own spiritual needs, as well as the spiritual needs of the group as a whole. But there is something further, especially if this shared prayer is done on a regular basis.

The teachers of our parish school of religion gather together after each class specifically for a prayer meeting. The system is utter simplicity. Someone reads a passage from the Bible, and makes his own comments on what it means to him. There is a period of silent reflection, during which anyone may add his own response. As simple as it is, it brings all of us the opportunity of sharing something of ourselves. There is yet something more. From this sharing comes a sense of closeness, intangible but real, impossible to describe, but felt by all. Here, especially, we are progressing beyond cooperation and sensitivity, to true community.

While all of this sounds beautiful and idealistic, we do have to face some practical questions. What about those who are unwilling to cooperate? What about personality conflicts? A basic truth concerning personal relationships comes to our rescue here, and that is that in any difference with another, *we* cannot change *them*. We can, however, change, or perhaps, control, our attitude toward them. First of all, we try to see others without criticism, trying to respect them as persons. In other words, see their good points, their dedication, their sincerity, their willingness to teach. That doesn't mean that we should stop trying to get them to cooperate, but we should continue to do so in a spirit of helpfulness. Personality conflicts are a little harder to resolve. Here perhaps all we can do is have a little calmness, and a great deal of good, old-fashioned Christian charity. Nor does any of this mean that the burden is entirely ours, but we do have to be willing to share our part of it.

So far we have been discussing community as it applies to all members of the program. There are, as we know, however, many different roles within the program; priests, director, principal, teachers, secretaries, aides. It is an easy thing for all of us, in our own special role, to forget the importance of others, who, though in different roles, are working for the same purpose. This purpose we may never lose sight of — to be formed personally in Christ more and more, and to work to form Christ more and more in others. There are two aspects that we may discuss.

First, let's take a look at ourselves. We have been called by God, remember, for a very special task. To this call we have responded, overcoming, by so doing, every objection and fear that besets us. We have brought to our task a dedication, a dedication of our time and talents, a dedication to a divine purpose. The role we have is a part — to be sure, only a part — but a part of the whole, just the same. We should be conscious, therefore, that what we do is important, to us, to the program, to those whom we serve.

At the same time it is important that we see the role of others. In the same way as we did, they have received their own call from God, and respond to it as generously as we have. They bring to their task a dedication similar to our own, and sometimes a dedication that surpasses ours. Since we are working with a total program, there is not really an unimportant job, although there are some that require more skills. All of this we know — we just have to keep reminding ourselves of it. There doesn't have to be conflict, you know, between people in different roles, but a conflict sometimes does occur. Call it the human side, if you will, but we do forget the importance and dedication of others. We must go right back to the fundamental principle of relationship — see the other person, not just what he is doing, and see him as one seeking to please God.

We may now discuss some individual relationships, in particular, the relationship of directors of the program to the teachers, and the teachers to the directors. The biggest mistake we make in our role of directors is to set up a program with all its rules, and make it as binding as the decalogue. More than any others in the program, we are the ones who have to see those whom we direct as people dedicated to the divine call. It is not easy, sometimes, to look past — or even overlook — the personalities of our teachers, for example, to overlook their teaching abilities, their methods, even their attitude to their students. While not letting glaring mistakes in these things occur, we do have to respect them as persons dedicated to the call from God. While this ideal of respect for the person runs like a thread through the whole pattern of personal relationships, there are some practical things which can help put everything together. Here are a few we have found helpful in our program.

First of all, we must keep in mind this most obvious fact, that the greatest majority of our teachers are "amateurs," non-professionals, and come to the program in the beginning with no formal teacher training. What they need most is *help*. Perhaps we could institute some sort of course on our own, for our own teachers. Hopefully, a more extensive course is available, through which our new teachers may come to at least basic skills. But as we know, the learning process is a continuing thing, and so is the teaching process. We may never stop improving, never stop becoming more effective teachers, both from "book-learning" and from experience. Hopefully, there will be available to us continuing opportunities for constant growth.

Encouragement, again especially for new teachers, is as necessary as the air we breathe. If we take the word encourage in its primary meaning, it comes out "enhearten," strengthen the heart, and in reverse, free from being disheartened, discouraged. Discouragement is as personal as our preferences, so therefore, is our need for encouragement as personal. One would think that as directors, we have to be practicing psychologists to relate to the variety of needs of all of the different teachers. Psychologists or not, that is just what we have to do, be willing to relate to each one of them as individuals. In this relationship, above all others, we have to see and respond to the "need of the moment." Obviously, these needs take many forms, and involve many different actions.

The first of these actions is giving direction. Here we may apply a rule found helpful by religious superiors, *direct firmly in love*. Show them the way, show them what is right, and insist that until a better method comes along, this is how a certain thing is to be done. This may apply to teaching methods, the presentation of truth, class disciplipe, taking care of problems, relationship with parents or the students themselves. Whatever it is, we direct them firmly, conscious of their need, always aware of them as persons, always in a spirit of true Christian love. Sounds great, but can we do it? We can if we have the right intention, if we are truly seeking their good, and not just getting something "off our chest."

At this point, we may say something about correcting mistakes. Some mistakes are of little consequence, or more or less general, and we may perhaps try to correct them in a general way, as for instance, in a meeting. Some, however, are little more serious, and personal, and we may be faced with the need of speaking to the individual. There is a rule in the officers' handbook of the U.S. Navy that we could apply here, "Praise in public, reprimand in private." Above all else, save the person the embarassment of letting others know. It takes some kind of a genius in personal relationship, really, to be able to correct another

without their being resentful, but this is what we have
to try to do. Again, "direct firmly in love."

Another way to increase good-relationship of
director and teacher is the personal interview. Ideally,
this should be done with any new teacher as soon as he
joins the program. It is helpful for all the teachers,
however, and perhaps could be used at the beginning of
the year with all as a matter of policy. It has the
immediate advantage of establishing open communication, especially with the new teachers. It also gives the
director the opportunity to point out what is expected
of the teachers.

To be really effective, however, the interview should
be a lot more than just reading many rules and
regulations. Ideally, it should be conducted on a
counselling level, with the new teacher doing most of
the talking, and the director responding with understanding. For the teacher it is the reassurance that he
is accepted and understood as a person. For the director,
it is an opportunity to learn something of the person —
the personal qualities — and needs — of the new
teacher.

There is one final duty of the director that at first
might seem insignificant, and perhaps not even worth
mentioning. This is just to be there. Be available. Come
early and stay on the job for the whole time of the
teaching period. Talking to teachers, from places where
the director stays "on the job," and where he does not, I
can say that this one thing, far from being insignificant,
is the most important thing he can do. Somehow or
other, there is a vast assurance that comes from his "just
being there."

There are a couple of personal qualities that are
helpful, almost necessary for directors of religious
education programs, both in relationship with teachers
and students. One is a spirit of openness, that quality

that is apparent to all that we are ready and willing to respond to them at any time, even if all they need is a piece of chalk. It helps if we have a natural tendency to this spirit of openness, but whether we do or not, we ought to see the need.

Secondly, we positively have to have a sense of humor. There is no substitue for this. In the best run program, there are too many personalities, too many problems, too many unpredictables, for us to react too seriously toward all of them. There just have to be times when the incongruity of the whole thing comes to the surface. At those times, we ought to be able to let ourselves go and laugh, even, or especially, at ourselves.

Summing all this up, we see that as directors, we need at least three degrees; administration, education, and psychology. In all seriousness, we do need to establish a balance between a well run program and happy people. These are not all contradictory, nor should they even be in conflict. At the same time, I personally feel that should there be any conflict, people count, not rules. Jesus himself said as much, "the sabbath was made for man, not man for the sabbath" (Mk 2:27). At the risk of being self-contradictory, we may, however, go back to our basic rule as directors, "Direct firmly in love."

Looking back on my own relationship with my former superiors, pastors, for example, and principals of schools, I have to admit honestly that my attitude was one of a fear that was a little more real than reverential. It really is too bad if we as teachers have a fear of those in charge of the program, for any reason whatsoever. We must admit that the fault could be partially at least with the directors, who seem to be more concerned with rules than people. But to be honest, a part of it is our fault, as well, if we fail to see them in their proper light. I would like to think that we see them as dedicated as we are ourselves, that their primary interest is that all those in the program, themselves, the teachers, and the students grow progressively in Christ. If we can have this attitude, then we will find it easy, or at least easier, to accept direction as it is given.

If we look at the whole program as a cohesive unit, with a single purpose or goal, we have to see that there must be one person in charge, to direct everything and everyone to that goal. For this reason, that one person is responsible for unity and order in the program. Former president Harry Truman had a sign on his desk that read, "The buck stops here." That is how it has to be. The other side of the coin, therefore, is respect for that order — in plain English, obedience. Obedience, therefore, is *not* a "dirty" word, but the realization of the relationship between two responsibilities, that of directing and that of accepting direction.

Returning to the idea first formulated, that we ought to see superiors as truly dedicated persons, we ought to have the confidence to go to them for assistance, in any need that we have. Sometimes we get the idea that asking for help is an admission of failure, or even lack of competence, but this need not be so. It is hard to ask for help, especially from those over us, but sometimes they are the most qualified to give it. Hopefully, they will also be the most ready. Once again, the attitude most needed here is confidence.

Finally, we need to want to help. This may sound superfluous after what we have already said, but not really. What we are implying here is not the mere compliance with all the "rules," but the extra spirit of willingness to want to make everything run smoothly. There is something more involved here. It means the active intention to go out of our way to do whatever is necessary to make things easy for everyone concerned. This is a part of our own dedication, and it begins with an attitude of awareness of the dedication of others, and a spirit of helpfulness in ourselves.

From here it is an easy step to review our relationship with others in the program, especially other teachers. Two qualities have to be present. We must have a true spirit of cooperation, conscious of the fact that we are all working for Christ, and for the formation of him in ourselves and others. Secondly, we ought to be free from all self-seeking. Of all the freedoms, this is perhaps the most important, and the last one we acquire. The most important because we can never truly relate to others unless we are free from selfish desires. It is easily the last to be acquired, because self does not die. There is a beautiful prayer in the "big book" of *Alcoholics Anonymous*, "relieve me of the bondage to self" (p. 63). We could make this prayer our own — say it and try to mean it.

All of this may sound idealistic, but there are three things we may keep in mind. First of all, the ideal is valid. As high and lofty, therefore, as it is, it is still attainable. That is not to say that it is attainable with ease, but just that it is attainable. None of us even pretends to be perfect, or hopes to be either, but we do have to be willing to grow along the lines that lead to a more perfect conformity with our ideals. Secondly, there is one Lord and Master of us all, no matter who or what we are. This is God, who is not so much Lord and Master as he is our loving Father. It is he who has called us, to him we respond, him we seek to please, toward him we tend. And finally, we look to Jesus, Son of God and our Model. He is the model of acceptance, having redeemed us through his full acceptance of the will of his Father. He is the model teacher, who not in word but in action, has taught us the true meaning of love and sacrifice.

CHAPTER VI
FOR WHOM ARE WE CALLED?

I have made your name known
to those you gave me out of the world.
These men you gave me were yours;
they have kept your word.
Now they realize
that all you gave me comes from you.
I entrusted to them
the message you entrusted to me,
and they received it.
They have known in truth that I
  came from you,
they have believed it was you who sent me.
For these I pray —
not for the world
but for these you have given me
for they are really yours.
I do not pray for them alone.
I pray for those who will believe in
me through their word,
that all may be one
as you, Father, are in me, and I in you;
I pray that they may be (one) in us,
that the world may believe that
  you sent me (Jn 17: 6-9; 20-21).

"I do not pray for (my disciples) alone. I pray also
for those who will believe in me through their word,
that they all may be one, as you, Father are in me, and I

in you; I pray that they may be (one) in us, that the world may believe that you sent me" (Jn 17: 20-21). These words from the Gospel of St. John were spoken by Jesus as a part of the prayer for his disciples, at the Last Supper. They tell us, in effect, that Jesus intended that his message of salvation should be passed down, one generation to the next, with the hope that all men eventually should come to the truth. We have come to this truth through those who have believed and have taught us. We now who believe must accept the duty and the challenge to communicate it to our children.

As we know, however, the teaching of religion is more than just the teaching of "catechism," enabling children to answer a bunch of questions, much as we teach spelling or the rules of grammar. Religious education is the communication of Christ, the whole Christ to the whole person. And once more with feeling, we cannot give what we do not have. We must form Christ in ourselves. But this is not a job we finish, as we do washing the dishes or writing a letter. Forming Christ in ourselves is a process, an ever growing process by which we continuously tend to be more perfectly one with him.

We tend to be one with Christ through personal goodness. But for us to want goodness, there has to be something attractive in it, we have to see a beauty in it. We find beauty in goodness when we find truth. Our intellect is our highest faculty, and the intellect of itself tends to the truth, and is satisfied only with truth. The more clearly we see the truth that Christ is the center and model of our lives, the more clearly we see the beauty of goodness, and the evil of sin. To see the beauty of truth and goodness, and to help our students to see it also, is one specific aim of Christian education. Perhaps, too, another way of saying that we must form Christ in our students is to say that we must form them into mature Christians. There are many qualities that go to make up a mature Christian. First of all, the quality of being able to see past the apparent value of purely material things to see the real value of spiritual things, to see the real value for example, of being of service to others, in contrast to seeking what we want for ourselves. In this connection, I always like to tell young people who are planning a career to seek to do more than just "make money." Seek to be educated in a field wherein you can be of service to others.

The second point in maturity is to be able to stand up for what we know is right. There are times in our modern materialistic culture, when just to be a Christian we have to be a hero. The pressure of peer groups, or what we call human respect, is indeed great, possibly more so on young people today than ever it was on us of the older generation. A young man or a young woman grows up fast when he is able to stand up to the challenge of sticking by what is right in the face of solid pressure to do wrong. Thirdly, maturity is the quality of accepting the responsibility of ourselves. Not just, therefore, being responsible persons, but accepting our own personal responsibility for ourselves and for what we have done. Particularly, to admit we have been wrong without excuse or alibi is one of the true marks of maturity.

In the actual process of communicating Christ to our young people, there are several attitudes we ought to take, several aspects we ought to see them under. The first of these is that we ought to take them where they are. Not all of them, perhaps not any of them have anywhere near the enthusiasm for Christ that we have. Not only that, a good portion of them come from families who lack any real enthusiasm for Christ. Very often we find children coming from families where one of the parents at least has little or even no faith at all. On the opposite end of the spectrum, we find children whose family background is one that is full of faith and devotion. More significantly, however, we find most of them coming from families of every shade or degree of difference between the two. We find the children coming from every degree of personal faith and personal devotion. This is especially true of students of the upper-grades and junior high. There is a big stretch of difference in the amount of Catholic truth that they have already acquired. This is easy to understand. Their background is every degree of Christian committment. Their previous religious education varies from daily instruction in a Catholic school, to weekly instruction, to nothing. Add to this the natural difference in the students ability to learn. Add also to this the difference in their willingness to learn, which varies from avid desire to complete indifference. We have to understand that many of these students are there only because their parents have sent them, and that they are giving up some of their free time, time when others of their age are playing football or jacks, or are watching cartoons on television. We not only have to cope with all of these differences, we also have to teach the students besides! Sometimes it looks like an insurmountable task.

Here is where we need the wisdom of the Holy Spirit himself to see what we are about. First and foremost, we must have the insight to see that we are teaching children, not just a subject. We must, therefore, have the willingness to try to respond to the individual needs of each member of the class, and this we ought to do on two levels. The first is the level of the whole reason why we are there, of communicating Christian truth, and the second is the level of personal need. To do this, we must see each one of our students as a person.

In the communication of truth or knowledge, we are taking for granted that our classes are interesting and well prepared. There is absolutely no substitute for this. But because we have to cope with a great variation in the students' present state of knowledge, there are a few qualities we could try to cultivate. We need a great amount of patience to enable us to explain, and explain again and again, if necessary to accomodate the degrees in the ability to learn. Sometimes we have to be aware of some individual's need, especially, for example, one who is too timid to ask. Above all else, we have to avoid being discouraged. This is an extremely easy piece of advice to give, but when we have seen a well prepared lesson plan utterly destroyed by our need to explain the background, perhaps, that we took for granted the students knew, or by the persistent questions of one kid who seems bent upon sinking the whole operation, such advice is a little harder to follow. Even so, we can avoid being discouraged if we keep in mind what we are about, the communication of Christ, and that we need to look at the whole picture, not just the details. We are doing God's work, and in spite of our apparent failures, we are making progress. We ought to have patience, forebearance and willingness to see and respond to each child's individual level of learning.

More important than responding to each student's educational need, is the desire to see and respond to each one's personal need. Each student has the need of being responded to as a person. We run into all sorts of hindrances on this one, most of them coming from our own personal reactions to the various individuals in our class. It is easy to respond to, to relate to, to feel close to the smart one, the interested ones, the ones who follow the lesson and take active part in the discussions. It is easy to respond to the appealing one, the blue-eyed blonde who never answers a question, but instead turns on a dazzling smile. It is a little more difficult, however, to have any personal feeling, except perhaps rejection, toward the slow and the sloppy or the one who has a positive genius for side-tracking and ultimately wrecking the whole lesson. It is, moreover, hard not to be disturbed, upset, and angry with the one who disrupts the lesson with all the annoying things that destroy our concentration; talking, playing, or just plain inattention. It is sometimes hard to remember that we have quiet ones in the class, who never respond, but just sit quietly and follow along. It is hard to remember, in fact, that they are even there.

Each of these we must see as a person. To each of these we must respond as a person. It would help if we could see Christ in each of them. Better if we could see each one of them in Christ, and in so doing seek to fulfill the need of each.

Our natural tendency in solving these difficulties brought on by the different personalities in our class is to try to keep everything in order, putting down the perpetual inquirer, and enforcing strict discipline on the one who disrupts the order. The motivation is clear enough. We are sure that the most important thing is to establish and maintain what is best for the class. There are times, however, when the question we must ask ourselves is not, "What is best for the class?" but "What is the best for this individual person?" Once again it may help us if we could see Christ in each of our students, and respond to them as we would to Christ. In any event, we have to see each of them as persons, individual persons, each with his own specific personal need, to which we ought to be able to respond individually. No one says this is easy. It helps to remember that our greatest influence on our students is not what we teach them, *but what we as persons bring to their lives.*

I remember an incident of my own. One of our seventh grade teachers had to quit with about six weeks of the year remaining, and rather than to find a substitute, I took over the class. There were three students, two boys and a girl, who were absolutely dedicated to preventing me from teaching anything. I won't go into details — let me just say that the class was one continuous interruption. After about two evenings of this, I was so incensed that I was determined to call their parents and tell them to keep them home and educate them themselves, I couldn't cope with them. In church the next morning, I was thinking about the situation, and I am sure it was the Lord who spoke to me, "You are *their* pastor, too." So I kept them. I can't remember how the rest of the year went, but I don't think it was too bad.

We have said that the teaching of religion is more than just teaching "catechism," or the communication of facts, or even of the truths of faith, but the formation of Christ in the hearts and minds of the students. At the same time, the beginning of this formation is knowledge of Christ, and so we begin with the communication of divine truth. Since, however, we must have knowledge to communicate, we may never stop trying to learn and understand better the divine truth ourselves. We must never stop studying, for example, never stop reading the Bible, never stop pondering over and meditating on the meaning of the truth for ourselves. Having ingested and digested this truth, we must seek the best ways to present it to our students so that they will be able to grasp it more, that they will want it. For this reason, a part of our role as teachers is to try to present the truth in as interesting a way as possible, so that we may capture and hold the interest of our students. But more than this, we must constantly seek better and better ways to present it lucidly, so that their minds may understand, and that they may comprehend not only the truth, but the inherent beauty of it.

An important part of the communication of Christ is to encourage a personal relationship with him. Thus we say, we need to teach our students to pray. But it is not all that simple. We can teach prayer forms, but not how to pray. The reasons for this is that prayer is communication, real personal communication with God himself. Since it is communication between ourselves and God, much of the intensity of prayer comes from God himself. Prayer is a gift, the gift of God coming to us. To this gift we respond, at the deepest level of our persons. At the same time, we can teach our students "how to pray," and we can and should teach them prayer forms. This is what Jesus did when the disciples asked him "how to pray." He taught them the familiar and beautiful "Our Father" (Lk 11: 1-4). We may teach various prayer forms as a part of our class, as the opening and closing prayers. A simple and effective method of teaching "meditation," for example, would be to use as a closing prayer some point in the lesson. We have the students think about that particular point in the relation to themselves and God, giving them a few moments to do so; we suggest a short prayer concerning it, again allowing a few moments; then we suggest something they can do, some resolution. The formula for the meditation is therefore; think; pray; do.

We may put all of this together by saying that what we need to communicate is "Christian awareness." Christian awareness — what Christ means to us, and how we ought to respond to that meaning. In a sense, this can mean the whole history of salvation, the whole relationship of God to man. God created rational creatures, men and angels, for his own glory, but also by the compelling force of his love, that sought to share his infinite goodness. So that man might know of God, his intimate nature, his fulfilling love, he spoke to him in the process that we call revelation. This process reached its perfect peak in the person of Jesus, the Son of God, who became one of us. Jesus is the revelation of the Father, the living communication of divine love.

The communication of God to man, however, is not just a universal thing, but a personal thing. God intends to establish a relationship with each one of us in person. Thus we may say that we have been called into existence by a specific and individual act of divine love. Each one of us, therefore, is not only individual to God, but sacred to God. Having created us out of love, he loves us with a love that is as eternal and without change as he is. Everything that comes to us in our lives, therefore, is nothing but the effect of the outpouring of his love. And since he has created us in his image, immortal in spirit, our final destiny is the realization of that love in all its fullness.

We see this relationship as yet more intimate when we say that God shares his life with us. God gave us the gift of life, human life, that is, since man came into being as man when God "blew into his nostrils the breath of life, and so man became a living being" (Gn 2:7). But there is more; Jesus brought us the fullness of divine life. "I came that they might have life, and have it to the full" (Jn 10:10). It is through this life that we are drawn to God, and drawn to God we are. There is in us a yearning for goodness, for happiness, for God himself.

The end result of all of this is, of course, our response. As teachers seeking to communicate Christ, we seek equally to communicate our response to him. This is first of all a response in faith, that deep faith in the assurance of God's presence, and his abiding goodness and grace in every part of our lives. We communicate also our response in goodness, demonstrated by the active intention, not just a wishful desire, to do all things to please God. Since the real essence of love is in sharing, our perfect response to God's love is to share it with others. God made us out of love, and gave us the freedom to love him in return, but not in any selfish or exclusive way. God is most pleased when, having shared his love with us, we share it with others, the same as we are pleased when, having been given a gift, the recipient shares it in turn. We may use the image of a stone thrown into a pool of quiet water. The ripples start in the center, and continue ever outward. They never come back. So also with the love of God. It starts with the gift of himself; it comes to us, to be shared with others, then others, and others, and others.

As we bring these thoughts to mind, sometimes the whole process of communicating Christ to others seems like a tremendous impossibility. But we may come back to two familiar ideas. First we recall that all we need to communicate is the gift of God in us that we have received. Secondly, since the whole thing starts with God, we may depend upon his grace. To depend on his grace sounds like a panacea at times, but there is nothing more true, nothing more real, than God's grace. It is for this that we have been called, to bring Christ to others. Since this call comes directly from God, we may have full confidence that his grace to fulfill all which that call demands will not be lacking. On God we depend, therefore, not on ourselves.

In addition, we must not forget that our young people have been called by God as surely as we have. They have been called to faith, to goodness, to live Christ. At times they may seem indifferent to that call, they may even seem to resist it, but it is there just the same. We might be tempted to think that this call is a sort of automatic thing, hereditary, as it were, involving exclusively the children whose parents are practicing Catholics. This is true of the largest portion, but not true of all without exception. By way of illustration, in our parish, each year for the past several years, there have been from eight to twelve young people, fifth grade to high school, who have started instructions and received the sacraments. For the most part, these have come from hitherto rather indifferent families. Some have come from non-Catholic families, and for a variety of reasons — most frequently through their friendships — have become interested in the Catholic Church. It is easy to see the special call to faith that these children have received. Every child, of whatever background, has been called, individually, and personally, just as we have received God's grace which has accompanied our call, so have they. We may have full confidence, that the grace to live their call will not be lacking to them.

But that is not all. We know that God sends his grace through others. This truth, in fact, is the whole reason why we believe that we have a special call. We know, we witness the fact that grace is communicated from parents to children. Not nearly as often, but often enough, the reverse process takes place. This is true in some of the instances we have mentioned above. It is through the faith of the children that the faith in the parents is born or re-born. Who can doubt that the providence of God is at work?

Among those whom God has designated to be his instruments, the pastor of the parish takes the first place. He has, in fact, been called by God specifically to form Christ in others. Simply as pastor, he assumes many different roles in the pursuit of his vocation. This is no less true of his relationship with the parish school of religion. He is called upon for things as divergent as solving a problem in theology, visiting a family whose children have stopped coming, and getting a new child to the right classroom. His essential tasks can, however, be broken down into three.

First and foremost, he is a priest. As priest, he fulfills all the basic sacramental and liturgical functions that belong to the priestly office. He offers the Mass, both for students and teachers, he hears their confessions, he presides at para-liturgical services, and gives the homilies. As priest-pastor, he is the primary representative of the bishop, and as such, the primary proclaimer of the word of God. In this role, therefore, he is teacher-guide to the teachers, the one to whom they may come for assistance in any doctrinal matter. As priest, last but not least, he must be available for personal spiritual guidance for anyone in the program, teachers and students alike.

Secondly, he is the director of the whole program. On him rests the responsibility for the success of the program in every department. Since, however, the actual operation of the program is the immediate responsibility of the Parish Religious Education Director, he works in close relationship with him. His role, however, is not "rubber-stamp" approval; it is consultative and directive, and at times, decisive.

The priest is a teacher. Next to the offering of the holy Sacrifice of the Mass, the most important thing the priest does is to proclaim the word of God. For this reason, he comes to each classroom of the P.S.R. on a regular basis. When he comes, he teaches definitively, from his special background in theology and from his experience. More than this, as any teacher, he brings himself to the students, who see him as teacher, as one interested in them as persons. The value of the priest in this role in no way can be underestimated.

I remember a priest in my own life. He was assistant in our parish during my grade school years. He made himself close to all of us, doing such divergent things as teaching religion in our classroom and umpiring our ball games. He was a poor umpire, by the way. I still recall my resentment when he called me out on strikes on three high pitches! I don't remember what he taught when he came into our classroom, but I do remember his teaching, and I do remember that it was he who gave me my first thought and inspiration about priesthood. He had the quality, so much talked about today, of being able to "relate." He gave us himself, and we all still remember him for that gift.

The simplest role of the priest in the religious education program, however, is to be present, just to be there. By the fact of his presence alone he gives all, administrators, teachers, secretaries, and aides, the assurance not only that he is interested, but that he supports them in every way. By his very presence he shows his readiness and willingness to assist in anything that may come up. Further, he is able to communicate to the teachers especially that their efforts are not only appreciated but are truly valuable for the children of the parish. If all he did was just "be there," he would be giving a service for which there is no substitute

In summary, therefore, we as teachers first and foremost bring Christ to our students. We do this by communicating the sublime truths of our faith, combining the truth of the message with the best possible teaching methods. We communicate the value of goodness, basing the need for it on the moral law as given by God, but strengthening its value by the fact that through goodness we establish a perfect relationship with others. We strengthen this communication of goodness, moreover, when by our own lives, by our example, we show them honesty, truthfulness and concern for others. We bring them closer to God when in our own prayer life we show a sincere devotion and confidence in God's goodness. In other words, and more importantly, we show them who we are. We show them ourselves, persons sincerely dedicated to God and his service, and to helping them form Christ in themselves.

CHAPTER VII
BORN TO NEW LIFE

God put Abraham to the test. He called to him, "Abraham!" "Ready!" he replied. Then God said: "Take your son, Isaac, your only one, whom you love, and go to the land of Moriah. There you shall offer him up as a holocaust on a height that I will point out to you." Thereupon Abraham took the wood for the holocaust and laid it on Isaac's shoulders, while he himself carried the fire and the knife. As the two walked together, Isaac spoke to his father Abraham: "Father!" he said. "Yes, son," he replied. Isaac continued, "Here are the fire and the wood, but where is the sheep for the holocaust?" "Son," Abraham answered, "God himself will provide the sheep for the holocaust." Then the two continued going forward (Gn 22: 1-2, 6-8).

In summarizing some of the important points that we have set down in the earlier chapters, we can first say the whole thing starts with God himself. We have not chosen him, he has chosen us. God has called us to the special task of teaching religion, of bringing Christ to others. We have seen and we believe that this is a call as personal and unique as God's call to Abraham, Moses, the Blessed Mother, the Apostles, and any of the others we have read about in sacred scripture.

Secondly, we realize that God calls us for his own

special purpose. That purpose involves our own relationship with God, not only our salvation, the ultimate purpose of our lives, but that through this call we might begin to live closer to him, in devotion, in love. Thus, we say that this call is a part of divine providence, not just in the sense that God's goodness is in every part of our lives, but in the special sense that he has planned for us a grace not given to everyone. At the same time, since his plan is not only salvation but increasing goodness for everyone, he has also planned that the call he gives to us be of benefit to all those whose lives we affect by our teaching. In other words, God has willed to use us for the continuation of good in the world.

Above all other things, however, God's call is a call of love. In the mysterious depths of divine providence, God has determined that we should be the recipients of his special love, in the form of enlightenment and grace. Again, therefore, we see this call as a special gift from God. But, as we may recall, God never gives anyone a grace for themselves alone. It has always been a part of the divine goodness to intend that any grace given be shared with others. We ourselves have experienced this, by the fact that much, if not most, of the goodness in our lives has come through others, by their encouragement and example. This is certainly true of God's love. In no way should it stop with us. As the gift of God has been freely given to us, so he intends us freely to share it with others. More than anything else, this tells us the true nature of our own call.

The significance of all of this is that it points out for us what it means to be a Christian. There are many definitions of Christian, actually, but certainly a valid one is a person who strives to be like Christ, whose life is patterned after that of Christ. The most notable characteristic of the life of Christ is that he fulfilled his

Father's will perfectly. So, this is where we begin, in this same intention, to fulfill the will of God. But we must follow Christ not only in the fulfillment of God's will, but in the whole pattern of his life.

If we look at the life of Christ, we may distinguish these three elements. First, here is the acceptance of his Father's will, next, the actual carrying out of it, right up to death itself, and finally, the joy of fulfillment in the resurrection. Vatican II points out to us that the redemptive act of Jesus involved the whole of the incarnation, his life, death, and resurrection. At the same time, the actual death of Jesus is the focal point of it all, the one act that everything led up to, and from which all else flows. Without denying that the crucifixion was the focal *action*, the focal *intention* took place in Gethsemane. Here Jesus, faced with the intense sufferings of his coming passion and death, weighed down with the burden of being man's single redeemer, in the depth of his humanity, besought the Father to let "this chalice pass." His final prayer, however, was, "Let not my will but yours be done" (Lk 22: 42). It is notable that he rose from that prayer, and showed not a single further sign of resistance, uttered not a single word of protest or complaint.

While all of this is true, Jesus really did undergo his passion, he really did suffer and die the intense agony of the cross. No one can possibly appreciate the intensity of Jesus' passion and death. And yet there was a triumph there, not only by the fact that sin and death were overcome, but by the fact that this death was the mark, the symbol, the prototype for all to follow — all who willingly die in some way to themselves, to bring about the kingdom of God.

Above all else, Jesus rose from the dead. In that resurrection, we not only see that triumph over sin and death, but the stamp of approval by God himself on the whole redemptive act. Suffering has no meaning by itself; it only has meaning in relationship to life. Jesus could look forward to the passion and death. He could also look forward to his resurrection, and surely it was this vision that sustained him in his darkest hour.

Without stretching our imagination one little bit, we can see in our call to be teachers the reflection of Jesus' life, death, and resurrection. In faith we are convinced that the Father has called us as surely as he sent his son into the world. And as Jesus answered his Father's call, by the incarnation, we have also, by our willingness to serve. We, too, have suffered the agony of fear and uncertainty. But we are sustained, as was Jesus, with the certain knowledge that we are doing God's will. And there have been times when we have felt our own personal crucifixion! The times when a carefully prepared lesson plan seemed to fall apart into little pieces; the times when we brought our students to a school assembly, or liturgical service, and were ashamed at their conduct; the times when the whole class turned into a disciplinary problem; the times we tried to get a troubled youngster to confide in us and we were rebuffed, and ended up in a state of frustration

Through it all, however, we are sustained. We are sustained by the conviction that this is all a part of an act of real love that we make, an act of love in response to the love God has shown us. Real love is never easy, if we look at it from the standpoint of giving. This is so because the very definition of love is the sacrifice of ourselves, the total gift of ourselves to another. But again, this is our gift to God, and it has many facets.

It is a gift of obedience. We may go back once again to the story of Abraham. Once he was sure of God's will, his obedience was complete. This was true of all those God called in the past. To a very high degree, this is also true of us. We have, however reluctantly in the beginning, accepted God's call. Basically, too, we have done so mindful of God's love and goodness to us. In a true sense, therefore, has our obedience been a sign and testimony of our love.

It is also a gift of trust. We have been sure that not only has God called us, but that he will be the source of all the help we need, and so we may trust him completely. We may recall the story of Abraham and Isaac as they climbed the mountain of sacrifice together. Abraham had said nothing about the nature of the sacrifice, to his wife, to the servants, to Isaac. Isaac, on the other hand, was fully aware of the practice of human sacrifice, since it was practiced frequently among the Canaanites. We note the urgency in the conversation:

"Isaac spoke to his father Abraham:

'Father!' he said.

'Yes, son,' he replied. Isaac continued,

'Here are the fire and wood, but where is the sheep for the holocaust?'

'Son.' Abraham answered, 'God himself will provide the sheep for the holocaust' " (Gn 22: 7-8).

It is quite possible that Isaac was not fully convinced, yet he continued up the mountain with his father, confident that his father would not deceive him. And of course, Abraham's words were truly prophetic, because God permitted him to substitute a ram found caught in the brush for his son.

This is a beautiful story of trust, a trust in his father's concern in the face of every indication to the contrary. This, of course, is the kind of trust we may have in God, a trust based simply on the assurance of his goodness. Trust of this magnitude, indeed, is an act of love, a gift of ourselves.

Our response is a gift of willingness. In a sense, we turn our lives and our wills over to the care of God, letting him make the final decision about which way we must go. There is a real gift here, in the sense of something freely offered, because to give our will is to give our one free faculty. There is an added value here, however, in this, that as we permit ourselves to be directed by God, we place ourselves under the care of divine wisdom, divine goodness, divine love. To do this fully, perhaps, requires a prayer, a prayer simple in its expression, but powerful in its meaning. We ask that God will grant us only this, the knowledge of his will, and the power to carry it out.

All of this means sacrifice, and this is likewise our gift. St. Ignatius, in his *Spiritual Exercises*, speaks about three levels of what he calls humility, but what we may call sacrifice or even love. The first is that of the normal good Christian, who is really willing to give up all things, including life itself, rather than commit serious or mortal sin. Keep in mind that this is not just a wish, but a positive will. The second level is that of the Christian who is striving to attain a little greater "perfection," who truly desires, and sincerely works for, full freedom from all deliberate venial sin. He is aware, of course, that for this he needs a special gift of the grace of God, because we are all prone to some sins, at least of indifference. But he prays for this grace, and seeks to cooperate with it. To attain this, he willingly accepts all that God sends him. The third level carries him right out of himself. He not only accepts willingly all that God sends, but he desires the cross, knowing that he must conform to Christ as perfectly as possible. We stand back in awe at a desire of perfection as complete as this, knowing that we are a long way from making such a commitment. There is in us, at the same time, a willingness to sacrifice. It is the sacrifice of accepting God's call, and the sacrifice of accepting all that comes with it. It is a sacrifice of generosity; it is a sacrifice of love.

God calls us for ourselves, because he wants to give us a gift. This is true of every call that God makes, and his gift is an interior peace, a true peace of mind. This peace has many aspects: calmness, contentment, personal satisfaction. All of these come to us directly through our accepting God's call. There is a calmness, a peace of conscience, simply from knowing that we are pleasing God. Nothing, by the way, destroys our peace of conscience quicker or more completely than a sense of guilt. On the contrary, therefore, we may be content within ourselves that we have accepted what we know to be God's call.

There is a marvelous satisfaction in leading others to God. This comes from the very nature of love itself. Love is self-diffusive, that is, by its own nature it seeks to go out from itself to others. We see this in the infinite love of God, which is the pure and total gift of itself. We have received this love in the form of God's goodness, and we experience it in the personal satisfaction of being close to him. By the very nature of this goodness that we have received, we get an immense satisfaction, a great pleasure, in communicating it to others.

Along with this, there is the satisfaction of accomplishing something worthwhile. This is not a negligible thing in any undertaking, and in teaching, it becomes a very important thing. This is all the more true because many of us started out with no previous experience in teaching, and some of us with a bare minimum of training. From those first nervous, uncertain days, when we were so unsure of ourselves, our students, and what we were teaching, that we faced every class with something like panic, we have progressed to a state of quiet confidence. And whereas before, in our near panic we never were sure of what we were accomplishing, now in our confidence we have the time and opportunity to see the progress our students are making. There is no thrill quite like that which comes when a student answers a question from a previous lesson, or when in the course of an explanation, a light comes to one of them and right in the middle of it, he says, suddenly and out loud, "O yeah!"

Above all else, is the personal spiritual values we have received. Really, it would be hard to enumerate all of them, especially since each of us has received them individually and in our own measure. But surely, these are among them. By the very task of teaching, we have received a wider comprehension of the truths of our faith. This is a natural result, first of all, of our study. In order to teach, we have to know, and in order to know, we have to study. But there is a special value in teaching, that comes from the very act itself. By the very fact that we have to present the truth to others in words, and especially by the fact that we have to make the matter clear, we fix it firmly in our own minds. We forget a lot of what we have learned, but we almost never forget what we have taught.

Our own faith has increased in strength and firmness. This, too, comes from our own deep desire to communicate it. Seeing the need for God in the lives of our students, we begin to see more clearly the need for God in our own. All of this makes us draw closer to him. Seeing the magnitude of the task, and our own inadequacies, more clearly, in fact, as we go along, we just have to turn to him in prayer. We pray indeed for ourselves, and especially because of our need to communicate him more perfectly to others.

Finally, we turn to God in gratitude. No one but ourselves can know the magnitude or value of his gift to us. This, then, is our resurrection. In the image of

Christ, we have been called to do God's will, we have been called to and have endured sacrifice, but we have been blessed with abundant joy. The God of love has called us, and he has given us his love. The God of peace has called us, that we might share more abundantly in his peace.